Our
High
Calling

*Practical and Devotional Thoughts
on Personal Sanctification*

Books by J. Sidlow Baxter

Awake, My Heart
Does God Still Guide?
Explore the Book
Mark These Men
The Strategic Grasp of the Bible

The Christian Sanctification Series

A New Call to Holiness
His Deeper Work in Us
Our High Calling

Our High Calling

*Practical and Devotional Thoughts
on Personal Sanctification*

J. Sidlow Baxter

kregel
PUBLICATIONS

Grand Rapids, MI 49501

Our High Calling by J. Sidlow Baxter.

Copyright © 1967 by J. Sidlow Baxter.

Publisher's Preface copyright © 1993 by Kregel Publications.

Published in 1993 by Kregel Publications, a division of Kregel, Inc., P.O. Box 2607, Grand Rapids, MI 49501.

Cover Photograph: K. G. Melde
Cover Design: Alan G. Hartman

Library of Congress Cataloging-in-Publication Data
Baxter, J. Sidlow (James Sidlow)
  Our high calling: practical and devotional thoughts on personal sanctification / J. Sidlow Baxter.
      p. cm.   (Christian Sanctification Series)
    Originally published: London: Marshall, Morgan & Scott, c1967.
    1. Sanctification. I. Title. II. Series: Baxter, J. Sidlow (James Sidlow). Christian Sanctification Series.
BT765.B36   1993   234'.8—dc20   93-13810
                                                          CIP
  ISBN 0-8254-2171-3 (paperback)

        1 2 3 4 5 Printing / Year 97 96 95 94 93

Printed in the United States of America

CONTENTS

PUBLISHER'S PREFACE

Although this exposition on biblical sanctification is a complete study in itself, it is also the third volume of the three-part "Christian Sanctification Series" by Dr. J. Sidlow Baxter. Included in this series are volume one, *A New Call to Holiness*, and volume two, *His Deeper Work in Us*, both available from Kregel Publications.

In volume one, *A New Call to Holiness*, Dr. Baxter sets forth the Bible's teaching on personal holiness and sanctification, emphasizing the believer's daily need to pursue the "deeper life" of holy living despite the pressures and busy schedules of modern life. Guarding against extreme positions and keeping his central question in focus—What is holiness?—he examines the relevant biblical passages on sanctification and applies them to the believer's daily experience.

His Deeper Work in Us explores the Bible's teaching on personal holiness and sanctification, emphasizing the "how-to" of entering into the experience and growth of inward sanctification. Some important questions addressed in this volume include: Does the Bible teach a deeper work of the Holy Spirit in the believer? What is the nature of inward holiness? How is it effected within us? Is there complete freedom from sin?

Dr. J. Sidlow Baxter completes this series in *Our High Calling* as he examines the Bible's teaching on personal holiness and sanctification, emphasizing the believer's daily need to completely surrender to Christ, hour by hour and even minute by minute. How does sanctification become a reality? Dr. Baxter describes the process: "As heart and mind become filled with love, all the *motives* become pure; and when all the motives are pure, that is *blamelessness*, and such moral blamelessness is true *holiness*."

Although Dr. Baxter makes numerous references to the testimony of Christian experience, his final court of appeal is always the Scriptures. For many Christian readers, hungering and thirsting after true holiness, these studies may well be a Jordan-crossing into the spiritual Canaan of biblical sanctification.

FOREWORD

NOT long ago I noticed a publication bearing the caption, *Recall to Sanity*. I immediately fell to considering how needful is such a recall in this nervous, palpitating machine-age of ours, with its wheels and wings, its wars and woes, its hyper-tensions and soothing pills. Then, by an easy, almost inevitable transition, my thoughts began relating it all to the churches, especially those which are still evangelical; and I found myself commenting, "If the world needs a recall to *sanity*, how urgently do the churches today need another recall to *sanctity*!" Fuel was thereby added to my fervent longing that the companies of our Lord's people might be set aglow again by a revived experience of Spirit-wrought sanctification. This, in turn, led to my preparing the expositions which now appear in this book.

Who will deny the need for a recall to sanctification? Travel among the churches (as has been my own privilege these last few years, in various countries, especially the North American continent) and what do you find? Generally speaking, among the officialdoms and churches of the major Protestant denominations, the witness to Scriptural holiness seems to have almost expired. The Methodists, who owe their corporate historical existence to the Wesleyan doctrine of salvation and sanctification, no longer bear resemblance to their venerable founder. Instead of likeness to him there is glaring contrast, at least so far as one may judge from some of their leading spokesmen. Especially among the Methodists in America, so it seems to me, many of the leaders and ministers, having jettisoned traditional Methodist theology, now wistfully blurr the "kingdom of heaven" into something like a Christianized Socialism. Being wiser than Wesley, they become the naïve but seemingly humanitarian tools of an anti-democratic ideology which, if it ever captures America, will strangle Christianity altogether. I hope I am wrong; but am I?

Of course, men of the "liberal theology" and transient "Neo-Orthodox" schools cannot be expected to hold traditionally Protestant or literally Biblical views on sanctification. Meanwhile, as one theological school or phase after another rises, attracts, disturbs, declines, and passes (as the older schools of "higher criticism" did, although supposed to be the last word), the Bible remains, ever-abiding and unchanged, with its clear, divine message to the wayfaring and simplehearted. The tragedy is, that while many of us ministers are under diverting spells of new schools and phases, men and women in their tens of thousands are denied the teaching of pure *Biblical* theology on the eternal salvation and present sanctification of the individual human soul. In this age of totalitarianism and collectivisms the big issue is the individual versus the mass-man. The first message of the Bible, and especially of the Gospel, is ever to the individual. It is time that we Evangelicals got back to preaching not only justification, but the practical *sanctification* of the individual through the provisions of the New Covenant. Is there not indeed new need today for a *recall to sanctity*?

As for this little book, whether few or many read it, of this I am sure, that its modest contribution is carefully Scriptural, and indulges no hyper-emphases. Its recalls were prepared as a series for preaching rather than as a treatise for printing; therefore, although there is little actual repetition in the successive addresses, there are recurrent references to certain *aspects* which would have been grouped together if the work had been originally prepared as a book. To some readers, however, its present arrangement may be advantageous rather than otherwise. It makes the treatment less formal, without being any less methodical, and gives added warmth without any loss of depth. May the dear Lord who is "made unto us wisdom, even righteousness and sanctification and redemption", be pleased to bless these pages to every reader.

J.S.B.

Our High Calling

*Practical and Devotional Thoughts
on Personal Sanctification*

DEDICATION

Spurred by memories of long and loyal friend-
ship, this book is dedicated to

JAMES COSSAR, F.C.A., F.S.C.,

of Edinburgh, Scotland ; my staunch companion
through shine and shadow ; and ever as warm
in heart as he is valiant for the truth.

Part One
Aspects of Sanctification

NOTE

Part one of this treatise is designedly as simple as we can possibly make it, for we earnestly desire that even the newest Christian believers may easily grasp the *positive* aspects of sanctification here presented. Part two is necessarily somewhat more involved, with maybe even an occasional touch of abstruseness, because we are there controverting what we believe to be sincere errors. It is part *one* which we are the more anxious to "put over" to those who seek the truth about sanctification, and we suggest that part two should not be read by younger believers until part one has been thoroughly digested.

J.S.B.

SANCTIFICATION:
ITS TWO MAIN ASPECTS

SOME years ago, as I was coming out of a so-called "Higher Life" meeting, I overheard an enthusiastic young lady accost an elderly man with the question, "Brother, are you saved?" to which he replied, "Yes, thank God, I know the Lord Jesus as my Saviour." Whereupon she hurled a second question: "But are you *sanctified*, as well?" which brought the further reply, "My dear young sister, I wish my answer could be as forthright as your asking, but most of us are still not sure what sanctification really is."

I am not sure whether I agree with the sharp-shooting of such questions at unknown persons. Maybe occasionally it is smart strategy, but more often it can be obnoxious. That to which I here call attention is the rejoinder, "Most of us are still not sure what sanctification really is". That speaks for many. Perhaps it represents some who read these pages. Indeed, that is why these chapters are written: they are intended for those who are "still not sure", but are longing for trustable information as to the possibility of holiness in heart and life. *What* is the sanctification to which our New Testament Scriptures repeatedly call us, allure us, exhort us?

"Sanctification" is one of the most resplendent words in our Christian vocabulary; and the New Testament *doctrine* of sanctification is one of the supreme distinctives of our Christian faith. Most, if not all, of the various groups or schools or bodies which have emphasized the importance and practicality of Scriptural holiness have taken that word, "sanctification" as their principal watchword or escutcheon.

Some groups have pretty well equated the word, "sanctification", with the *eradication* theory, i.e. the teaching that the hereditary sin-bent in our human nature may be excised or extirpated by spiritual surgery, or by an inward, simulated co-crucifixion with Christ. For instance, Dr. H. A. Ironside, in his *Holiness, the False and the True*, thus describes the earlier form of earnest holiness teachings which gripped him during his younger years: "In the merely justified soul there remains a corrupt principle, an evil tree, or 'a root of bitterness', which continually prompts to sin. . . . The *eradication* of this sinful root is *sanctification*" (42).

Dr. Ironside later repudiated this eradicationist misfeaturing of the word, as many others of us do; yet still today, whenever the word, "sanctification", is used, there are those who immediately think of it as meaning this supposed eradication of "inbred sin". Others use the word with a less radical connotation, though as often as not it is connected with some off-focus *theory* of holiness. Most of us realize that the word somehow represents a high level of Christian walk and experience, yet there are such misted notions of it floating round that many people in our churches seem to regard sanctification as a fad of peculiar minorities outside the regular Protestant or Evangelical denominations.

That such widespread misunderstanding should exist about the word and its meaning is a spiritual disaster. Millions of Christian believers live out their days on earth without ever knowing coherently what is the highest and richest spiritual provision for them in Christ during this present life. If there is one thing more than another which our evangelical churches are needing to hear just now, it is a ringing recall to Scriptural holiness; and if there is one New Testament term more than another which calls for rescue, it is that precious, expressive word, "sanctification".

Both the doctrine and the experience of Christian sanctification are of unspeakably sacred importance to every Christian; and it is our hope that this present catena of studies may possibly elucidate sanctification in such a way that at least some who read may, with clarified understanding, "go up" and "possess" the promised "inheritance" with its "fulness of blessing".

> Lo, Canaan's borders, open wide,
> For God's redeemed to dwell inside!
> Our Captain leads, and all may share
> The "fulness of the blessing" there.
>
> The clear-writ promises declare
> Our present heritage lies there—
> With mind and motives all renewed,
> And by His Spirit full-endued.

A rest, in Christ, from inner strife,
Through His infilling love and life ;
A present, inwrought holiness,
With Pentecostal fruitfulness !

Yet pilgrims hesitate and shrink
At Jordan's intervening brink ;
And ask : Does God indeed bestow
Such full salvation here below?

One simplifying distinction which we all need to make at the
outset is the difference between *positional* sanctification and *experiential* sanctification. Through confusing these, many have been
perplexed and hindered. They have found themselves asking, "If
the New Testament repeatedly says that in Christ we already *are*
sanctified, why does it equally urge us to *become* sanctified?"
The answer is, of course, that we already *are* sanctified in the
sight of God, by our new *standing* in Christ (i.e. "positional"
sanctification); but we are meant to become sanctified in heart
and life through the deeper ministry of the Holy Spirit *within* us
(i.e. "experiential" sanctification). Let us prise this open a little
further.

Wherever the words, "sanctify", "sanctified", "sanctifieth",
"sanctification", appear in our New Testament, they are always[1]
either verb forms or noun forms of the Greek adjective *hagios.*
That adjective, *hagios,* occurs no less than 278 times in the New
Testament, and is a wonderful study for all who have a mind to
explore it. However, lest we should frighten anyone away by
details of analysis or etymology in this opening study, I have
deferred all such to the end of the book, where the main meanings
and usage of *hagios* are given in a brief *Excursus on "Positional"
Sanctification.* According to preference, that excursus can be
consulted either now or later.

All we need say here about the *meaning* of the Greek word,
hagios, is that its primary idea was *separatedness,* from which there
later developed the further connotation of *purity,* inasmuch as all
those persons or articles which were separated for sacred purposes
had to undergo special cleansings. Those, then, are the two main
ideas of the Greek word which is translated as "sanctified" in our
English New Testament: (1) set-apartness, (2) cleansedness.

---

[1] That is in the Authorized (i.e. King James) Version; but the same is true of
the E.R.V. (English Revised Version), and the A.S.V. (American Standard
Version).

There are teachers who would have us strictly *limit* the meaning of the word, *hagios* ("sanctified"), to set-apartness, but are they right in so doing? Some 94 times our New Testament names the third member of the Godhead, the "*Holy* Spirit", each time using the neuter of *hagios*. Does it mean no more than "the set-apart Spirit"? Are we to read Romans 16: 16, "Salute one another with a set-apart kiss"? Do the words of 1 Peter 1: 15, "He who called you is holy", mean no more than that God is "set apart"? The holiness of God is His utter, infinite purity of character; and who would dare assert that the holiness of God is different in kind from the holiness which He requires in ourselves, except that the one is absolute and original, whereas the other is relative and inwrought?

Evidence is abundant all over the New Testament that sanctification or holiness in a Christian sense means an inward, moral, spiritual *purity*. That is what all of us Christians long to know more about. Does our New Testament really teach the possibility of an *inwrought* heart-purity, a renewal of our whole moral being by the Holy Spirit?

Well, as we have just remarked, the first basically important feature to observe is, that all the many New Testament references to the sanctification of believers break up into those two main categories: (1) *positional* sanctification, (2) *experiential* sanctification. Positional sanctification is objective: something wrought *for* us by God through Christ. Experiential sanctification is subjective: something wrought *in* us by God the Holy Spirit.

POSITIONAL SANCTIFICATION

So far as our *positional* sanctification in Christ is concerned, perhaps all we need do here is refer to just one of the various passages which teach it. (For others see *Excursus*.) A remarkable representative is Hebrews 10: 10,

"By which will [of God] we *have been* sanctified through the offering of the body of Jesus Christ *once for all*."

Notice carefully that the verb here is in the perfect tense, which denotes an act already completed: "we *have been* sanctified." Notice further that the self-offering of our Lord, through *which* we "have been sanctified" was "*once for all*". As the offering was "once for all", so is the sanctification which it effected for us. This clearly must mean *positional* sanctification. Through the perfect character and perfect sacrifice of our dear Lord, and His perfect coverage of all our demerit, we have been once-for-all and for evermore sanctified before the eyes of God.

This statement of our once-for-all positional sanctification in Christ is all the more noteworthy because only four verses later we have an equally arresting reference to an intended *progressive* sanctification in our present *experience*. See verse 14 which, when its present passive participle is more strictly translated, reads:

"For by one offering He [Christ] has perfected *for ever* those who *are being* sanctified."

So, very definitely, in that one paragraph, both these two basic aspects of sanctification are differentiated for us. We *"have been* sanctified" "once for all" and "perfected for ever" (positional sanctification), but also, as a present parallel and counterpart of that, we are now *"being* sanctified" (experiential sanctification).

The following simple abstract may usefully crystallise the leading New Testament references to *positional* sanctification.

1. It is by election of God the Father
   (1 Pet. 1: 2 ; Heb. 10: 10).
2. It is through union with God the Son
   (1 Cor. 1: 2 and 1: 30).
3. It is actualised by the Holy Spirit
   (2 Thess. 2: 13 ; 1 Pet. 1: 2).
4. It is coincident with justification
   (1 Cor. 6: 11 ; Acts 26: 18).
5. It covers all believers collectively
   (Acts 20: 32, 26: 18).
6. It is once for all, perfect, for ever
   (Heb. 10: 10, 14 ; 2 Thess. 2: 13).

How wonderful is this *positional* sanctification! Dear Christian believer, let it not be said that you or I ever read or think about it without an exulting gratitude to our infinite heavenly Father from whose boundless grace and wisdom it comes to us. Oh, the deep and precious wonder of it! Travel back in mind through the B.C. centuries, and gaze again on Israel's first high priest, in his adornments of "glory and beauty" (Exod. 28: 2). See those two gems, one on each shoulder-piece of the ephod, each inscribed with six of the Israel tribe-names. See those other twelve precious stones in the breastplate, each gleaming jewel bearing the name of one tribe. Then reflect again that it is all pictorially anticipative of our glorious Lord Jesus and His redeemed people.

As you see Aaron wearing that golden crown imprinted with *HOLINESS TO THE LORD,* and those resplendent robes adorned with those memorial jewels on his shoulders and on his heart, you are seeing a typical (though necessarily inadequate) likeness to *our* Great High Priest as He represents us yonder, before the Throne of the heavenly Majesty. Our holy God sees you and me in *Him*—in His exquisite "beauty of holiness", in His robes of unsullied sanctification, in the gleaming loveliness of His utter purity and moral splendour, and in those opalescent jewels which shine with our names on His mighty shoulders and on His tender heart!

That is what our "positional" sanctification means! Wonderful as is our justification in Christ, our positional sanctification in Him is surpassingly so. Our new standing of justification in Christ means that God, our holy Judge, now sees us to be as legally faultless as our sinless Sin-bearer Himself, whose imputed righteousness now covers us. Sinlessness, however, by itself is negative; it is the *absence* of all legal culpability and moral ugliness; whereas sanctification, or holiness, is positive: it is the *presence* of moral loveliness. God now sees me in Christ not only as justified, but as sanctified, i.e. not only (negatively) as being sinless in the sinlessness of Christ, but (positively) as made beautiful in the very loveliness of Jesus Himself!

> Near unto God am I,
>   Nearer I cannot be ;
> For in the person of His Son
>   I am as near as He.
>
> Dear unto God am I,
>   Dearer I cannot be ;
> For in the person of His Son
>   I am as dear as He.

Never-ending wonder! Thank God, it is true and *more* ; for our positional sanctification in Christ spells out a further strophe:

> Cleansed before God am I,
>   Purer I cannot be ;
> For now the *loveliness* of Christ
>   Completely covers me!

Such indeed is the gracious contrivance of divine love and wisdom! Certainly, the first meaning in our positional sanctification is that of set-apartness to God, but the further truth is that the heavenly Father now sees us in the all-perfect *loveliness* of Christ, the Beloved. And, if that is how God now sees us, ought not our most sacred ambition be to live in suchwise as answers to that astonishing marvel of divine "kindness toward us"? I could scarcely believe my own ears, some time ago, when I heard two members of a certain very orthodox sect arguing that because God always sees us as "perfect in Christ Jesus" it does not matter in the least what our actual behaviour is! They had it off in pat phrases, too. "Our *state* does not affect our *standing*." "What we are in *self* has nothing to do with what we are in *Christ*." One wonders how such diseased thoughts can germinate in the hearts of the professedly regenerate—on which, however, we shall have further comment in a later chapter. Let it be the undying passion of our regenerated hearts that our "state" shall as nearly as possible reflect our "standing", and that our *positional* sanctification in Christ may be paralleled by a true sanctification of *character*.

EXPERIENTIAL SANCTIFICATION

Let us now gratefully turn our minds to what the New Testament teaches concerning *practical* sanctification in the life and experience of Christian believers. There is no need to quote here all the forty or more New Testament texts which directly refer to this, but the several which I here select exhibit its main aspects.[1] In some of them "sanctification" carries little more than its primary meaning of set-apartness, while in others it undeniably expresses a deep and decisive work of the Holy Spirit in the soul. Some texts show us that in sanctification (mark this well) there is a place for the exercise of human *endeavour* in co-operation with inward renewal by the Holy Spirit, whereas still other texts emphasize that the inwrought renovation is the work of God alone. Some passages seem to indicate an initial sanctification *crisis,* while others denote a sanctification *process*.

As an instance in which the word, "sanctification", is used with scarcely more than its primary meaning of set-apartness, glance

---

[1] For fuller comment on the meaning of "sanctification" see our Excursus on the *Etymology of Sanctification,* p. 203.

at 1 Corinthians 7: 14, "For the unbelieving husband is sanctified [viewed as set apart] in the wife, and the unbelieving wife is sanctified in the husband". No inward change is implied in the unbeliever married to a Christian, but because the Christian wife or husband has dedicated *all* to Christ, including the marriage partner, the latter, too, is in that sense set apart. (See also Rom. 15: 16 and 1 Cor. 3: 17.)

In contrast, such verses as Ephesians 1: 4 indicate an *inward* sanctification or holiness which can mean nothing less than a deep-going renewal of our moral nature: "He [God] chose us in Him [Christ] before the foundation of the world, that we should be holy [sanctified] even *without blame* before Him, in love." (See also Col. 1: 22.)

Such inwrought experience of heart-holiness can be effected only by God Himself. Yet whatever gracious transformations it may beget within us, it never operates in such a way that we ourselves are thenceforth excused from all earnest strivings of our own to fulfil the divine ideal of sainthood. The Holy Spirit so renews us as to make moral and spiritual victory a dynamic reality, but He never exempts us from battle. There is a place for human response, resolution, effort; and any teaching of holiness which does not recognize this is not true to the full Scriptural data. When by our own eager response and free choice we become altogether "set apart" to Christ, He infuses a holiness which can make us "more than conquerors", and in a way never experienced before He companions us in all our encounters with temptation; but He never fights our battles *instead* of us, for that would frustrate their educative process after the pattern of our great Captain who Himself "suffered, being tempted" (Heb. 2: 18). Hence we have exhortations like 2 Corinthians 7: 1, "Let us cleanse *ourselves* from all defilement of flesh and spirit, completing [our] holiness [or sanctification] in the fear of God".

Yes, there is a place for co-operative response and endeavour on our own part. Only our Lord Himself can inwardly *change* us; we cannot change ourselves; yet there *is* something which we ourselves must do. There is to be our own accompanying self-separation; a voluntary, determined self-separation from all the doubtful and unworthy, as indicated in the text just quoted, and an earnest pursuit or "following after" *continuous* sanctification. That expression, "following after" is the very word used in

Hebrews 12: 14—"*Follow after* . . . the sanctification without which no man shall see the Lord."

The High Quest

Well, having thus (so we hope) made these several aspects of sanctification preliminarily distinct and clear, we may now devote our thinking specifically to the high quest and big question with which these pages are concerned. Our high quest is a genuine experience of inwrought sanctification. Our big question is: What does our New Testament teach concerning such sanctification and the way into it? Since we have now drawn the line so clearly between *positional* sanctification and *experiential* sanctification, let it be plainly understood that from this point onwards in these chapters, whenever we use the words, "sanctify", "sanctified", or "sanctification", we always mean sanctification in the inward, practical, *experiential* sense, unless stated otherwise.

In the remainder of this introductory study, let us focus our attention, even though very briefly, on just one verse of Scripture which makes a perfect lead-in to our theme. It is 1 Corinthians 1: 30, which in the King James Version reads as follows:

"But of Him [God] are ye in Christ Jesus, who of God is made unto us wisdom and righteousness and sanctification and redemption."

As the text thus reads, it teaches that Christ is "made unto us" a fourfold provision: (1) wisdom, (2) righteousness, (3) sanctification, (4) redemption. It is preferable, however, to read it as rendered in the English Revised Version or the American Standard Version or in other more recent translations, all of which separate "wisdom" from the other three items, so that the reading becomes,

"But of Him ye are in Christ Jesus, who has been made unto us wisdom from God, even righteousness and sanctification and redemption."

There can be little doubt that such is the intention of the original Greek. Over against the false wisdom of the "world", which the context here criticizes, God has given us Christ as the *true* wisdom, bringing "righteousness and sanctification and redemption".

I chatted recently with a student who thought it rather strange that this text should put "sanctification" before "redemption". Is not the true order, he asked, "redemption" first, through the precious blood; then "righteousness" second, through the risen Saviour; and then "sanctification" third, through the indwelling Holy Spirit? To my own mind, it is a risky business correcting Paul! He has a way of always turning out right. Undoubtedly our text puts things in the true order, for the simple reason that Paul here uses the word, "redemption" in its eschatological sense, that is, in the sense of yet future and final redemption, just as he does in Ephesians 4: 30, where he says that we are "sealed *unto* the day of redemption", or again in Romans 8: 23, where he describes us as "waiting for . . . the redemption of our *body*".

The fact is, these three words, "righteousness" and "sanctification" and "redemption", as used in our text, give us the three *tenses* of our salvation in Christ. First, there is the past tense: "righteousness" through what He once did *for* us on the Cross. Second, there is the present tense: "sanctification" through what He now does *in* us by the Holy Spirit. Third, there is the future tense: "redemption" in its eventual climax, which He will bring *to* us at His return in glory.

Now Paul's centering of "sanctification" here between "righteousness" and "redemption" is significant. Just as "righteousness" (i.e. justification) and "redemption" (present and future) become ours *by faith,* so does "sanctification" (inwrought and experiential). It comes, not by self-works, but through faith in Christ. It is psychologically axiomatic that self cannot *change* self; neither can self really *conquer* self. The struggle of self with itself, and the dismaying result, are graphically depicted in the "wretched man" of Romans 7. The more his higher self struggled, the more the lower self struggled, until the fundamental contrariety of his divided ego wrung from him the cry, "Oh, wretched man that I am! Who shall deliver me?" The picture is not overdrawn, as all of us know by experience, except the abnormally jejune among us. There is a continual civil war between the higher and the lower in us, between urges of good and urges of evil, both of the contending armies wanting to capture the resources of the one personality in which they campaign.

You and I cannot, of ourselves, change what we hereditarily *are*. We may discipline ourselves, religionise ourselves, chain, thrash, suppress, or cloister ourselves; but we cannot inwardly *change* ourselves. Any radical change within us, in our innate impulses and propensities, must be effected by a power from outside of us—a *divine* power, even the power of the Holy Spirit; and this, says the Word, is made ours in Christ, to be appropriated by consecrated hearts through *faith*.

Notice too, in the text, that our Lord Jesus has *"been made"* sanctification to us, which means that our sanctification is altogether in Him. Knowing that we ourselves could never restore our nature to holiness, God has *provided* holiness for us in and through His dear Son. This again underlines the fact that holiness is not *attained* by self-effort, but is *obtained* through appropriation of Christ. Perhaps the word, "obtained", may not be exactly the best, but it serves to emphasize that sanctification in its sense of inward renewal is something *received,* not something *achieved.* As truly as justification becomes ours through Christ *for* us on the Cross, so sanctification becomes ours through Christ *in* us by the heavenly Paraclete, the Holy Spirit.

May we not now, therefore, preliminarily commit ourselves to the following six cardinal propositions?

1. Inward, *experiential* sanctification is always to be distinguished from *positional* sanctification. It is imparted, subjective and progressive, whereas positional sanctification is imputed, objective and unchangeably perfect.

2. Inward, experiential sanctification is a renewal and renovation of our moral nature which only the Holy Spirit can effect within us.

3. This inward sanctification is a blessing to be received or appropriated by faith, in answer to our loving, adoring, self-yielding to Christ.

4. It is well to distinguish between sanctification and *entire* sanctification (1 Thess. 5: 23). Experiential sanctification begins with our regeneration at conversion to Christ, and from then onwards there may be *degrees* of inward renewal according to our measure of consecration to Christ; but *entire* sanctification, with its continuous *infilling* by the Holy Spirit and its deepmost renewal of our whole moral being comes only when there is an *uttermost* self-yielding to Christ.

5. *Entire* sanctification—as both Scripture and experience seem to make clear—is both a crisis and a process. We do not gradually grow into it, or slip into it, or get it piecemeal. There is a decisive initial crisis of utter self-yielding to Christ at all costs, with an accompanying utter reliance on the divine promise to make the blessing real; then a subsequent process in which the image of

Christ is ever more clearly stamped upon the now Spirit-filled personality.

6. There is a place for human will and effort. Although the human will can never rid the human self of hereditary, innate proclivities to sin, there is a whole area over which the will has control—choices, habits, friendships, ways of thinking, speaking, behaving; and throughout this whole region of our self-consciousness there must be a complete ejection of all known wrong, a continuing, adamant refusal of compromise, a daily walking according to the written Word, daily communing with God in prayer, and daily witnessing for Christ as discretion indicates.

We shall be touching on these six points again and again in the ensuing chapters, but even here, without further waiting, do we not with good reason *begin to interrogate ourselves*? I am truly converted, but am I truly consecrated? I now possess Christ, but do I let Him really possess *me*? I am spiritually regenerated, but am I morally *renewed*? I am "born" of the Spirit, but am I *filled* by the Spirit? I have the new life, but do I experience the "life *more abundant*"? I am into "the blessing of the Gospel", but do I have "the *fulness* of the blessing"? (Rom. 15: 29.) I am out of Egypt, but am I living in Canaan? I am "risen with Christ" (Eph. 2: 6), but am I "*reigning* with Christ"? (Rom. 5: 17.) I know Him as my imputed righteousness, but do I know Him as my *imparted holiness*? I know that I am saved by faith, but have I the experience of being "*sealed* by the Spirit"? I know that in Christ I am now a "child of God", but is my prayer-life a *filial fellowship* with the Father? I have "peace *with* God", but do I have peace *from* God filling my soul?

Oh, how big and blessed is God's giving! But how poor our responding and receiving! Are there not many of us groaning for deliverance from bondage to sin, yearning for a life of radiant victory, longing for inward purity, for a deep-going renewal by the Holy Spirit?

> Not merely pardon for my sins,
> But victory over *sin*,
> The very source where sin begins
> Renewed and cleansed within ;
> Not weary strugglings to repress,
> But all my mind renewed,
> Refined by inwrought holiness,
> Possessed, infilled, endued.

That is entire sanctification. That is the blessing we all need; and it is ours in Christ, who is "made unto us righteousness and sanctification and redemption". Let us "go up and possess", for God says, "Every place that the sole of your foot shall tread upon, that have I given you".

The land of promise gleams ahead,
  The Christian's highest quest;
Wherever faith shall firmly tread
  Is ours to be possessed:
Our Saviour's Calvary sacrifice
  Has made it yours and mine;
All now is ours by purchase-price
  And covenant divine

This is the promised inward rest
  Redeeming love provides;
How deeply, richly he is blest
  Who in its peace abides!
Here Spirit-filled believers find
  Full vict'ry over sin,
Complete renewing of the mind,
  True holiness within.

This is our true inheritance,
  Our heaven on earth below;
Must doubt or subtle circumstance
  For ever whisper, "No"?
Lord, help us grasp the promises
  And claim the inheritance,
And prove indeed how real it is
  In rich experience!

SANCTIFICATION:
CRISIS AND PROCESS

"When the hearts of converts are warm with their first love, then is the time to make them fully acquainted with their Saviour; to hold Him up in all His offices and relations, so as to break the power of every sin—to lead them to break off forever from all wrong self-dependence, and to receive Christ as a present, perfect, everlasting Saviour. . . . You might as well expect to roll back the waters of Niagara with your hand, as to stay the tide of their former habitudes of mind, surrounded as they are with temptation, unless they have a deep and thorough and sanctifying experience of the Saviour."

Charles G. Finney.

SANCTIFICATION:
CRISIS AND PROCESS

"The very God of peace sanctify you wholly ; and your whole
spirit and soul and body be preserved blameless unto the
coming of our Lord Jesus Christ" (1 Thess. 5: 23).

THE call to sanctification is one of the most ringing imperatives of
the New Testament. Because that is so, there devolves upon every
Christian believer the high obligation to ascertain what sanctification is, and to live in the reality of it. The text which we are here
to consider is a kind of standard-bearer for many other New
Testament verses which belong to this subject of sanctification.
Let me remind you of several.

"Sanctify them through Thy truth ; Thy word is truth" (John
17: 17).
"Christ also loved the church, and gave Himself for it ; that He might
sanctify and cleanse it with the washing of water by the word" (Eph.
5: 25, 26).
"For this is the will of God, even your sanctification . . . that every
one of you should know how to possess His vessel in sanctification and
honour" (1 Thess. 4: 3, 4).
"God hath from the beginning chosen you to salvation through
sanctification of the Spirit, and belief of the truth" (2 Thess. 2: 13).
"Follow after peace with all men, and the sanctification without
which no man shall see the Lord" (Heb. 12: 14, E.R.V.).

The New Testament teaches us that many of the Israelite ordinances and incidents described away back in Exodus, Leviticus
and Numbers, were advance types of spiritual truths pertaining to
the Christian Church. In certain remarkable ways, also, those old-
time Israelites themselves were types of us Christian believers.
How significant, therefore, for *us* are the words of Leviticus 20,
which solemnly declare God's priority requirement of His covenant people!

"I am JEHOVAH, your God, which have separated you from other
people."

"Ye shall be holy unto Me; for I, JEHOVAH, am holy, and have severed you from other people, that ye should be mine." "Sanctify yourselves therefore, and be ye holy; for I am JEHOVAH, your God" (Lev. 20: 24, 26, 27).

The New Testament echoes this in 1 Peter 1: 15, "But as He which hath called you is holy, so be ye holy in all manner of behaviour". The flagbearer verse, however, which lifts up together all the principle aspects of practical sanctification is the one which we have chosen as our text: "The very God of peace sanctify you wholly; and your whole spirit and soul and body be preserved blameless unto the coming of our Lord Jesus Christ."

First, then, let us learn what this text tells us as to the *nature* of sanctification. Often when we are exploring a New Testament text it is useful to go behind the English translation of it to the original Greek wording. In this case, however, we may learn much from our own English word, "sanctification", which is an excellent translation of the Greek original. Our word, "sanctification" comes from two Latin words—*sanctus*, which means "sacred" or "apart"; and *facio* which means "I make". So *sanctus* and *facio* together mean, "I make sacred", or "I set apart". That is the precise meaning of "sanctification". To be sanctified means to be set apart. In a Christian sense, it means to be set apart to Christ. In both the literal and the practical sense, entire sanctification is complete set-apartness to Christ.

This helps us to iron out some misunderstandings right away. Sanctification is not sinless perfection. There are persons in our churches who vociferously persist in the objection that when we urge sanctification we are preaching "sinless perfection", as they call it. That objection, however, is a product either of prejudice or of ignorance. The sanctification to which the Scripture calls here and now is voluntary set-apartness to Christ. There are others who seem to suppose that when we speak of being sanctified we are claiming a kind of Pharisaic spiritual superiority. There are still others who think that sanctification is a species of religious peculiarity, and that those who talk about being sanctified are to be avoided as spiritual extremists. Such objectors, however, have cause to be ashamed, for in unmistakable syllables the New Testament repeatedly calls the Christian believer to sanctification. We ought to get it clearly in mind, once for all, that sanctification is *not* sinless perfection; it is *not* a cliquish spiritual superiority-complex; it is *not* some peculiar slant or hyper-emphasis. It is a voluntary, practical set-apartness to Christ.

Let us not mystify ourselves, either, by thinking that sanctification is some hallowed, inner secret of the spiritually élite, or some recondite, elusive, heavenly-minded superiority which is only accessible to outstanding Bible students, or to the religiously cultured, or to the mystically minded, or to those who are far advanced in Christian knowledge, or to those who are enswathed by a kind of pious aura. No; as we keep saying, sanctification, according to the very etymology of the word, is set-apartness. Therefore, in its first practical *Christian* meaning, it is our sincere, willing, grateful self-yieldedness or set-apartness to God, to Christ, to the Holy Spirit.

But now, further, when we understand the word, "sanctification", in this way, it helps us to distinguish it from certain other experiences of the deeper Christian life with some of which it is often confused. Sanctification, on the human side, is not *in itself* the experience of being "filled with the Spirit". It is not, in itself, the promised experience of being "endued with power from on high". It is not, in itself, the experience of the Holy Spirit inwardly "witnessing" that we are "the children of God". It is not, in itself, the "higher life", or the "victorious life", or the "life more abundant", or an inwrought state of holiness, or any other post-conversion "further work of grace" in the Christian believer.

Sanctification is the set-apartness which makes all these possible. It is that which *leads* to them. It is the golden hinge on which all these blessings turn. When once we are sanctified, in the sense of a voluntary, whole-hearted set-apartness to Christ, then, and *only then,* can our dear Lord begin to make all these further and deeper experiences of the Christian life real to us. He never leaves a surrendered vessel empty. He redeemed us in order to possess us; and our sanctification, or set-apartness, makes His full occupancy of us possible. It is *then* that in the deeper sense He begins to fill us with the Spirit, to "endue" us with power, to make real in us the Spirit's "witness". It is *then* that He lifts us to the higher life "in heavenly places", the life of victory and abounding, the experience of inwrought holiness and conformity to His own pure likeness.

Another thing which becomes clear when we understand sanctification on the human side as a voluntary set-apartness to Christ is, that entire sanctification may begin with *the crisis-point of a moment*; for the instant that I become really and fully set apart to Christ I become entirely sanctified. It has nothing to do with any supposed inward, spiritual surgery by which the Holy Spirit cuts out a so-called "old nature" or "body of sin" in the believer. No; sanctification (let it be emphasized yet again) is this set-apartness to Christ; and it may therefore become effected by the pin-pointed transaction of a moment.

Of course, I would be the first to agree that sanctification is a *process* as well as a crisis; yet never can there be any unimpeded *process* of sanctification apart from this initial *crisis* of the moment by which we become *wholly* set apart to Christ. There may be a long, winding way, with many a hesitation, leading up to our act of self-dedication, but when at last we reach the point where we say with heart-deep meaning: O Saviour, I love Thee so deeply and so dearly that I give Thee my whole being utterly and forever, that very moment we become sanctified. After that, we are to *remain* set-apart, and thus the initial crisis introduces a subsequent progress.

One other thing which we ought to mention here about this beginning of sanctification is that there are *two sides* to it—a negative and a positive. We are to be set apart *from* sin, and set apart *to* Christ. These two aspects—the "from" and the "to" must always go together. There cannot be true separatedness to Christ without a true separatedness from sin. Does someone ask, "But how can I separate myself from those sinful inclinations and defilements which are a part of my inherited human nature?" The answer is: you *cannot* separate yourself from those. Only God can deal with such innate problems of our fallen creaturehood. When we talk about our separation from sin, we refer to all those things in our nature, in our habits, in our behaviour, in our self-expression, over which we ourselves have control as normal human beings. So far as our own choice and will and power to act are concerned, there must be a clean break from all known wrong in the life. *That* is something which we *can* do. Then there must be a complete yielding up of intellect, emotion, will, faculties, possessions and powers to Christ. Nothing less than that is sanctification; but once we are genuinely there (let us not hesitate to affirm it) we are *sanctified*; for what we really give to Christ, He really takes, and really counts as set-apart to Himself. Such, then, is the meaning of sanctification, as indicated by the word itself.

But now, if we consult our text again, we find that it indicates the *effect* of sanctification in the heart and life. It says, "Your whole spirit and soul and body be preserved *blameless*". That word, "blameless" is of key importance here. It is just as important in what it does *not* mean, as in what it *does* mean. Mark it well, our text does not speak of our being "preserved *faultless*". The illuminating word which it uses is "blameless".[1] There is a world of difference between faultlessness and blamelessness. The main difference is, that faultlessness has to do with our natural faculties, whereas blamelessness has to do with our *motives*. In this present life, while we occupy these mortal bodies, we shall never have faultless powers, either mental or physical. The infirmities of our fallen Adamic nature will cling around us until we are liberated by the supernalising translation which wings us into the presence of our heavenly King. When we are up yonder with Him in the glory, or are sharing with Him in His promised millennial reign, our completely reconstructed and glorified human nature will be faultless in every part of its triune territory—spirit, soul, body. But here and now, in this present permitted order of things, the Word of God does not call us to faultlessness: the clear and consistent call of the Christian Church Epistles is to *blamelessness*.

Now blamelessness, as I have already remarked, refers mainly, if not wholly, to our *motives*. When all the motives of my mind and heart, of my ambitions and purposes, of my speaking and doing, are cleansed and pure toward God, and toward all my fellow-creatures, that is blamelessness; and that is the first, big, deep-going blessing which sanctification makes possible.

But *how* does sanctification effect this inward cleansing and renewing into a condition of blamelessness? If we consult our text again, we find that the working of this lovely moral miracle is attributed exclusively to *God*. It is not something which *we* achieve by our voluntary set-apartness to Christ, or by any sort of ascetic rigour following our self-surrender. It is a result which God Himself effects in *response* to our yieldedness to Him. Our text reads, "The very God of peace sanctify you", which plainly indicates an activity of *God*. And again it says, "Your whole spirit and soul and body *be preserved* blameless"—which clearly implies something done *for* us, and not *by* us. Again, verse 24 adds, "Faithful is He that calleth you [to this] who [God] also will do it".

---

[1] We discuss in a later chapter the Greek words translated as "blameless".

The fact is, that when *we* set ourselves fully apart to Christ by our own voluntary choice, *He* sets us apart for the special ministry of the Holy Spirit within us. It is *then* that we begin to experience the meaning of verses like Romans 5: 5, "The love of God is shed abroad in our hearts by the Holy Spirit which is given unto us". It is then that in deeper reality the Holy Spirit begins to refine our desires and intents and inclinations. It is then that the mind of Christ thinks through *our* mind; that the will of Christ moves through *our* will; that the love of Christ expresses itself through *our* love; that the life of Christ lives through *our* life; that the compassions of Christ flow through *our* emotions; that the presence of Christ communicates itself through *our* presence. It is then that all the motives of the heart and mind become interpenetrated by the Holy Spirit, suffused by the love of Christ, renewed and sublimated, and made "blameless". It is then and thus that holiness is wrought in the believer by the infilling of this heaven-imparted life and love. It is not faultlessness, but *blamelessness*.

This brings us to a further arresting feature of our text, namely, the intended *extent* of this sanctification and blamelessness. Halt again at the words, "Your whole *spirit* and *soul* and *body* be preserved. . . ." With such explicit pronouncements as this in God's Word, there surely can be no doubt that our human nature is *tripartite*. We are not merely bipartite (mind and body), but *tri*partite (spirit and soul and body). The non-material or sentient part of us is distinguished into "spirit" and "soul". The distinction between spirit (*pneuma*) and soul (*pseuche*) is traceable all through Old and New Testaments. That the spirit and the soul are not identical is indicated, for instance, in the statement of Hebrews 4: 12, that God "divides" between them. By the body man has *world*-consciousness; by the soul *self*-consciousness; by the spirit *God*-consciousness.

There is a remarkable parallel between our threefold human constitution and the old Israelite tabernacle in the wilderness. The specifications and descriptions in Exodus tell us that the tabernacle was in three parts—(1) the outer court, (2) the holy place, (3) the holy of holies. The outer court was a quite spacious, oblong, rectangular enclosure, one hundred cubits long by fifty cubits wide; so, as the old Hebrew cubit was a little over one foot six inches, the outer court was approximately one hundred and fifty feet long by seventy-five feet wide. It was always erected with the two longer sides facing, respectively, northward and southward, so that the two ends of the width looked out, respectively, eastward and westward. The entrance was at the eastern end.

Inside that spacious enclosure, and toward the westerly end, was the "sanctuary" which housed the other two parts of the tabernacle. It was thirty cubits long by ten cubits wide, the longer sides again facing northward and southward, the front and rear eastward and westward, with the entrance at the eastern end. The "sanctuary" was in two compartments, the first twenty cubits comprising the "holy place", and the remaining ten cubits being the "holy of holies".

The entrance to the outer court was called the "gate". The entrance to the holy place was called the "door". The entrance to the holy of holies was called the "veil". The outer court was for the people. The holy place was for the priests. The holy of holies was exclusively for the high priest; and in that innermost shrine, the holy of holies, there continually flamed and flashed above the golden, cherub-guarded mercy seat, the wondrous, awful, supernatural glory-light called the "shekinah".

Observe, then, a few of the correspondences between that threefold Israelite tabernacle and our threefold human constitution. The outer court is the *body*; the holy place is the *soul*; the holy of holies is the *spirit*.

The outer court gave that old Israelite tabernacle its contact with this outward, visible world of mankind. The holy place was that part in which the central ministries of the tabernacle were daily performed. The holy of holies was that most sacred part of all, which gave that tabernacle its contact and communion with God. Similarly, in our threefold human constitution, the body, or outer court, is that which gives us our contact with the outward, visible, material world. The soul, or holy place, is the essential centre of human personality and consciousness, in which intellect (or reason) and volition (or free will) and emotion (or feeling) continually function. The spirit, which is our human holy of holies, is that which makes man *capax Dei*, "capable of God", giving us our capacity for God, and making possible our communion with Him.

Now one thing which cannot fail to impress us in that old Israelite tabernacle is, that the materials and adornments prescribed for the outer court were noticeably inferior to those which were prescribed for the "sanctuary", i.e. for the holy place and the holy of holies. The hangings of the outer court were of fine-twined linen, and the boards or wooden pillars were of acacia wood with fillets of silver and sockets of brass. In the *sanctuary* all the boards were overlaid with gold, the sockets were silver, and the hooks were gold. The curtains and hangings were of blue and purple and scarlet, decorated with cherubic figures and wrought with exquisite needlework. So is it in our threefold human tabernacle of spirit and soul and body. The spirit and soul are of finer texture and far greater value than the body. You would not think so from the usual television advertisement, or from the usual magazine article; but it *is* so. The body is exceedingly important, yet it is the least important, and therefore to live wholly or mainly for the body is a pathetic blunder with sad consequences which reach beyond the grave.

It is further observable that the outer court could be taken down without affecting the inner sanctuary consisting of holy place and holy of holies. Similarly, this outer court which we call the human body may be taken down, or discarded, at that strange dissolution which we call "death", without aborting or even interrupting the continuity of individual human personality and consciousness. That is so because the body is not the person. A human being *is* a sentient person, and that sentient person *has* a body; the body is a surround only, and not the essential.

Note again that although the outer court of the old Israelite tabernacle could be taken down without affecting the inner "sanctuary", yet the two parts of that inner sanctuary (the holy place and the holy of holies) could not be separated from each other. No; for although the holy place and the holy of holies were divided by the exquisite "veil", they were both parts of that one, dual, inner sanctuary. They could be distinguished, but not disjoined. Even so, the soul and the spirit of man may be distinguished, and to the eyes of God "divided asunder" (Heb. 4: 12, 13), but they cannot be disjoined into parted entities. The soul is the self-conscious human ego; the spirit is the God-conscious capacity which inseparably attaches to it, and is meant to give sacredness to the whole sanctuary of the human personality.

But we must by-pass other parallels in order to mention now the significant *final* parallel. There came a moment when all the required materials for that old-time Israelite tabernacle had been subscribed—the dyed flax of blue and purple and scarlet, the fine linen, the yarn of goats' hair, the stags' skins and "rams' skins dyed red", the acacia wood, the oil for the light, the spices for the incense, the onyx stones and other precious gems for the high priestly ephod and breastplate; the gold, the silver, the brass, bracelets, rings, earrings, jewels; and the variegated work had all been completed—pillars, sockets, hangings, curtains, bars, pins, and coupling rings; also the furniture, i.e. the brazen altar, the brazen laver, the table of shewbread, the seven-forked candle-stick, the golden altar of incense, the ark of the covenant, the cherub-guarded mercy seat; and there the new tabernacle now stood, erected at a cost of well over one million dollars.[1] The divine requirement now was that it should become completely *set apart,* or "sanctified"; and that indeed was what now took place.

See, then, what happened in that old Israelite tabernacle when it became entirely sanctified. Exodus 40: 34, says, "The glory of the Lord *covered* the tabernacle; and Moses was not able to enter the tent of the congregation because the cloud *abode thereon,* and the glory of the Lord *filled* the tabernacle". Just how the covering cloud of glory appeared to the thousands of Israel, who shall say this long while after? But it *did* appear, giving those long-ago Israelites visible evidence that their infinitely holy God, Jehovah, had now come to indwell that sanctuary in a hallowing way. So is it when you and I become really set apart to Christ. In the *spiritual* glory of His life and love He takes possession of the human personality—infilling, subduing, refining, enduing, illum-ining, ennobling, transforming the mind, by the Shekinah of the Holy Spirit, so that even the outer court, the face, the eyes, the looks, the expressions, the tones of voice, the whole bearing and behaviour begin to share in the hallowing experience. Thus is it that we become "sanctified wholly", and our whole "spirit and soul and body"—the whole human tabernacle, becomes pre-served "blameless" unto the "coming of our Lord Jesus Christ".

Years ago now, when my dear wife and I had gone to our ministry at Bethesda Free Church, Sunderland, away up the north-east coast of England, we began to hear lovely reminiscen-ces from the older members about a certain deacon of that church, who had died years earlier. We were told that wherever he visited, he left a fragrance of Christ; that if he happened to come upon a group of friends, the conversation immediately seemed lifted up to a higher plane; that if ever he was present it was difficult to gossip unkindly or criticise others; and that in the

---

[1] See Exodus 38: 24–26, where the Hebrew gold shekel equals about thirty dollars at present currency

deacons' meetings, if tensions were becoming acute, or tempers seemed frayed, or tongues were over-hasty, he would get up and say, "Brethren, may we just pray over this?" with the effect that by the end of the prayer the whole atmosphere was wonderfully congenial again! Oh, he left a lovely testimony! His name was W. T. Longstaff. Have you ever heard of him? No? Ah, I think you have. We often sing a hymn which he wrote; a hymn which he not only wrote with his pen, but exemplified in his life:

> Take time to be holy,
>   Speak oft with thy Lord.
> Abide in Him always,
>   And feed on His Word.
> Make friends of God's children;
>   Help those who are weak;
> Forgetting in nothing
>   His blessing to seek.
>
> Take time to be holy,
>   The world rushes on.
> Spend much time in secret
>   With Jesus alone.
> By looking to Jesus
>   Like Him thou shalt be;
> Thy friends in thy conduct
>   His likeness shall see.

I have sometimes heard that precious hymn criticised by persons who thought they "knew a thing or two" better than its author. I remember one preacher who disdainfully exclaimed, " 'Take time to be holy'? Nonsense! Take *Christ* to be holy!" Such supercilious word-smartness, other than exalting Christ, betrays a pitiful superficiality, and blurs the real issue. Certainly we must "take *Christ*" to be holy, but in this matter of initial sanctification followed by life-long holiness it takes *time* for us to take all of *Christ*. We cannot "get there" in five minutes, or by hurried snatches of prayer which are scarcely worthy of being called prayer. We need time to get really quiet, to get really alone with Jesus, to wait on Him, to listen to Him, to let Him search our hearts, and to deal with us as we need. We must "take time to be holy".

I heard another preacher say, "We may improve the wording of this hymn. Instead of singing, 'Take time to be holy', let us sing, 'Take time to *behold Him*'." It sounded such a Christ-honouring criticism; yet it was pathetically misguided. None would agree more eagerly than I that we are all needing to take more time in prayer to behold Him; yet even more important than our beholding Him is our becoming *like* Him. That is why, in the last glimpse which Scripture gives us of the glorified saints, it says, not only that they shall "see His face", but "His name shall be written *in their foreheads*"—that is, they will be so like Him, that when you look at *them,* you will see a reflection of *Him.* There can be *no* true likeness to Him without *holiness*; and there will be no such holiness unless we "spend much time in secret, with Jesus alone".

It "takes time" for most of us even to get ourselves to that initial crisis-choice where heart-holiness *begins*—that "cross-roads" of the will at which we take the way of utter self-abandonment to Christ. In my earlier Christian life, when I myself was wistfully seeking to know the reality of sanctification and its attendant results, I found my longings flowing out into a little hymn which I have preserved. Perhaps it may now become the language of some other seeking Christian heart. I invite you to pray two of the verses with me:

> Sanctify me wholly,
>   Sovereign Saviour mine ;
> Spirit, soul and body
>   Now make fully Thine.
> Make my motives blameless,
>   Purify my heart ;
> Set me now entirely
>   For Thyself apart.
>
> Here and now I yield, Lord,
>   Thine to be alone ;
> Now is "Self" uncrowned, Lord,
>   *Thou* dost take the throne.
> Ever keep and fill me,
>   Pour through me Thy grace ;
> Till, at Thine appearing,
>   I behold Thy face.

SANCTIFICATION:
WHY? WHAT? HOW?

"If a man is unwilling to give up his sins, to deny himself all ungodliness and every worldly lust, if he is unwilling to be *set apart wholly and forever* to the service of the Lord, he will either reject this doctrine [of sanctification] altogether, or only intellectually admit it, without receiving it into his heart. It is an eminently dangerous state of mind to assent to this, or to any other doctrine of the Gospel, and not honour it in practice."

Charles G. Finney.

SANCTIFICATION:
WHY? WHAT? HOW?

"For this is the will of God, even your sanctification"
(1 Thess. 4: 3).

As we read these words, the first thing which arrests the eye
and strikes the mind is, that sanctification is the plainly stated
"will of God" for us. We have good reason to reflect that the
words of this text are not merely those of a man; they are the
call of the Holy Spirit Himself through an inspired apostle. So
our text is indeed the voice of God about the *will* of God—the
will of God for all His redeemed people in Christ. "This is the
will of God, even your sanctification."

When the will of God is articulated so definitely and explicitly
about a matter, every truly Christian heart will surely give
earnest heed. Do I now happen to be addressing some professing
Christian who, because of conflicting theories or extremist views
of sanctification, is negligently ignoring it? If so, let me respectfully utter a rebuke. Dear Christian, redeemed by the precious
blood of Christ, in thus disregarding intelligent and practical
sanctification you are contradicting the directly revealed will of
God for you, and thereby grieving the Holy Spirit.

May I remind you that when the will of God is so openly and
decidedly expressed as it here is about our personal sanctification, our obedience becomes all the more emphatically a sacred
obligation. It follows, therefore, that if we are living an *un*sanctified life, even though professedly Christian, we cannot be fully
pleasing to God; nor can we enjoy the highest *blessing* of God;
nor can we know the richest *fellowship* with God; nor can we
be most *useful* to God. Furthermore, if we neglect the revealed
will of God as to this paramount concern of our sanctification,
how can we call ourselves followers of that dear Saviour and
Master who said, "My meat is to do the will of Him that sent
Me"?

"This is the will of God, even your sanctification." Because sanctification is so clearly revealed as the will of God, and because it is therefore a "categorical imperative" of the Christian life, there can be no *substitute* for it. No amount of attractive gifts, or of successful public ministry, or of outward religious correctness, or of symmetrical culture, or of giant intellect, or of wealth and generosity, or of social superiority and prestige, can be a make-do for sanctification. It is only when we are sanctified that we "walk in the light as He is in the light". It is only then that we develop a heart-to-heart fellowship with the heavenly Father and the exalted Son. Make no mistake about this: "sanctification" is one of the great words of the New Testament; it represents a real experience; an experience which is not only a practical possibility but a divinely-insisted necessity if, as Colossians 4: 12 says, we would "stand perfect and complete in all the will of God".

I must confess that at times my own spirit is jarred and grieved by the adroit casuistry with which certain Bible expositors of a sort *circumvent* this serious New Testament call to sanctification. There are those who say, in effect, "Oh, we need not be too disturbed about our *actual* sanctification; all Christian believers are *positionally* sanctified in Christ. Whatever kind of life we now live cannot impair our perfect standing of righteousness and sanctification in Him." Yes, that is their line; and a favourite text of theirs is Hebrews 10: 14, "For by one offering He hath perfected for ever them that are sanctified." It is sad that professing Bible teachers can deceive themselves and others by such subterfuges. We all thank God for our *positional* sanctification in Christ. We thank God that despite our unworthiness we are accepted of the Father in the representative, all-covering righteousness of the Son. But even though our "positional" sanctification in Christ covers our responsibility to the divine *Father,* what about our direct, individual responsibility to the divine *Son?* Who shall cover us from the holy anger of *His* wounded love, if we have dodged genuine sanctification here on earth by pretentious expedients or counterfeits? It is *He,* our holy Saviour, God the Son, who calls to us from our text: "This is the will of God, even your sanctification"; and we are each accountable to *Him.*

There are others who argue something like this: "Well, whatever we are here and now, whether individually sanctified or not, we need not worry overmuch; for when we leave the body, at death, and pass into the presence of the Lord, all sin is then utterly obliterated from our disembodied human nature. Otherwise, how could we enter heaven? We shall all be equally and perfectly sanctified then; so why worry overmuch about sanctification now?" To my own mind, such an assumption comes perilously close to implying that death can do something for us which the blood of Christ and the power of the Holy Spirit cannot. Yet surely one moment's clear thinking must convince us that the dissolution which we call death can have absolutely *no* power in itself to eradicate innate moral evil. If it had, would anyone ever pass through it into hades and judgment and Gehenna? Where is there any Scripture which says that death eradicates sin, or sanctifies us, or transforms us? Death is dissolution; but that dissolution is not moral transformation.

Let us settle it in our minds, once and for all: whatever moral and spiritual change may be wrought in Christian believers at their disembodiment, it is wrought solely and wholly by the Holy Spirit. Just what He then does, who on earth shall dogmatically declare? In times of revival the Holy Spirit has often come suddenly upon men and women with wonderful illuminating and transforming power; and this may well suggest an even more expansive and elevating sublimation just beyond death; but where Scripture is silent or reticent it is folly for us to presume. One thing *is* certain: there can be no such transformation for the knowingly disobedient or insincere; and, to my own thinking, it certainly savours of insincerity to know that the will of God is our present sanctification, yet try to evade it by round-about reasonings. Let us be frank: if we do not hate sin, and long to do the will of God, and yearn to please Him by a sanctified, Christ-possessed life, then we have cause enough to doubt the reality of our conversion. Death cannot sanctify the disobedient or insincere.

But I have heard others argue thus: "It cannot be *too* important whether or not we are sanctified here and now, because Jude's epistle tells us that in the ultimate consummation we shall *all* be 'presented *faultless* before the presence of His glory with exceeding joy'." Yes, thanks be to God, that also is true, though not perhaps in just the way that some dear brethren fore-picture it. All those who are then presented yonder will have been made perfect in their human *nature*—spirit, soul, body; but does the fact that they will all then be "faultless" in *nature* mean that they will all be equally elevated in *character?* Not at all! Our "nature" is the basic raw material; our "character" is what we *make* out of that raw material. Just as our conversion to Christ in this present life on earth affects the whole of our destiny hereafter, so the way we live *after* conversion, in this present life on earth, affects our *character* throughout the whole of the hereafter. Sickness, adversity, poverty, persecution, if endured prayerfully, resignedly, praisefully, can do something in our *character* to fit us for ministries in the heavenly realm; ministries which otherwise could never be ours. Everything in this present, mortal life is *significant* for that immortal life beyond. That is why, although all Christian believers will be saved, the Word of God distinguishes between "overcomers" and others; between some who have an "abundant entrance" and others who are only "saved, yet so as by fire".

To live a life of sanctification in this difficult "present world" does something in the *character* which makes us even dearer to the Lord who bought us, and fits us for special ministries by and by. It lifts us up into an innermost fellowship with our Lord in which He unveils His face to us as He cannot to others (John 14: 21; 2 Cor. 3: 18, 1 John 1: 7). It lifts us into the ranks of the overcomers. Mark it well: even in that "heavenly country" over yonder, "one star differeth from another star in glory". The Demases who have "loved this present world" rather than sanctification cannot hope to enjoy the rewards of the Pauls who were "vessels unto honour, sanctified, and meet for the Master's use" (2 Tim. 4: 10; 2: 21).

Let none of us ever doubt it again: sanctification here and now is of simply immeasurable consequence for that vast continuity beyond. Over against those who talk about "positional" sanctification as though it rendered *practical* sanctification unimportant, and over against those who talk about sanctification at death or at the final consummation as though it made *present* sanctification unnecessary, we place two solemn, unmistakable verses of Scripture. The first is Hebrews 12: 14, "Follow peace with all men, and the sanctification without which no man shall see the Lord." Quite plainly, *that* sanctification, "without which no man shall see the Lord", is something which is to be "followed" here and now; not postponed until death! The other verse is our text, 1 Thessalonians 4: 3, "This is the will of God, even your sanctification, that every one of you should know how to possess his vessel in sanctification and honour". We hold the trumpet to our lips again, and sound the divine clarion to all Christian believers: "THIS IS THE WILL OF GOD, EVEN YOUR SANCTIFICATION."

At this point let me underscore a fact about which there seems hazy doubt. It needs to be emphasized repeatedly. Sanctification in its inward, experiential sense really *does* something inside the moral nature of the consecrated believer. It is not *only* a self-yielding on the human side, nor merely a "reckoning" ourselves sanctified in the sense of set-apartness. It is a divinely effected *renewal* of our thought-life.

In the days of my youth, soon after my conversion to Christ, I became keenly enthused by the overflowing holiness meetings which used to be held in many centres about that time. There were the usual two main schools of teaching on sanctification: (1) the eradicationists, who taught that there are "two natures" in the believer, i.e. the evil "old nature" and the unsinning "new nature", and that sanctification comes by the eradication of the "old"; (2) the counteractionists, who objected to the eradicationists and insisted that although the "old nature" could be "crucified" it nevertheless remains alive within us to the end of our earthly days.

Between the two teachings some of us felt sore perplexity. We wanted to "go all the way with Scripture", as the eradicationists exhorted, yet we feared to presume *beyond* Scripture as we listened to the warnings of the counteractionists.

But the outstanding feature was that *both* schools equally firmly preached sanctification as a work so deep and radical in the believer's moral nature that it well merited being called distinctively "the *second* blessing". We need to recapture this truth that real sanctification *does* that big something within us: and if we ask *what* it is that is divinely inwrought, we may crystallize it into threefold definiteness as something: (1) imparted, (2) effected, (3) attested.

Something Imparted

First there is that which is *imparted*. In some quarters today there is a teaching that only those believers have the Holy Spirit who have had the so-called "baptism and speaking in tongues". How such misinstruction can gain ground against plain Scripture to the contrary is one of many mysteries. All true believers are

"*born*" of the Spirit (John 3: 6, 1 John 5: 1). All such have new
spiritual *life* (John 3: 36, Rom. 8: 10, 1 John 5: 12). All such
are indwelt by Christ through the Spirit (John 14: 16, 20, Rom.
8: 10, 1 John 3: 24).

Yet although all born-again Christians "have" the Spirit, do
they all experience the *fulness* of the Spirit? By general admission
the reply is a disappointing "No". Does the New Testament anywhere *teach* that all the born again are filled with the Holy Spirit?
It does not. Does it teach that all the born again *may* be? Apparently so, for without discrimination the Epistles encourage and
exhort believers to the experience of it. Nowadays, to many professing Christians, such an infilling is merely wistful theory, and
the idea of one's whole life being lived continuously in this fulness
seems a fond illusion. Such doubt is easy these days, surrounded
as we are by anti-God philosophies and widely prevailing material-
istic attitudes. But the blessing is none the less real; and the cure
for suspicious doubt is to get our minds fixed on the written Word.
As a greatly used servant of our Lord said to me some time ago,
"Almost to the last I was pestered by doubt and tricked into
hesitancy, but when eventually I let the unfaltering voice of the
New Testament drown out other voices I sought the blessing in
downright earnestness, and soon afterward I knew the exuberant
reality of it. Since then my whole experience of God has been on
a sunlit higher level. I never guessed until then that there could
be such rapturous interchange between God and a human heart
this side of heaven".

Perhaps, indeed, that is the most *predominant* registration of
the infilling in our human consciousness—a vivid, new awareness
of the heavenly Father and the risen Saviour. Not always is there
emotional exhilaration. That is one of the more variable acci-
dentals. But spiritual realities become lucidly clear and lumin-
ously present to the mind. With an insight higher than comes by
human logic we really "*know*"—know with new and thrilling
aliveness to it that we are truly "redeemed with the precious
blood of Christ"; that we are "born from above"; that the Father
and the Son and the Holy Spirit *love* us; and that our risen Lord
personally indwells us. It was to this kind of supernaturally in-
duced "knowing" that our Lord referred when, in telling the
disciples what would happen when the Spirit came upon them,
He said, "At that day ye shall *KNOW* that I am in the Father,
and ye in Me, and *I in you*" (John 14: 20). When the Spirit

actually filled them, oh, how vividly they *knew*! They knew God, and the risen Lord, and the authenticity of the Gospel, in a way which no Christian apologetics or religious science could ever convey!

However, without lingering over different aspects of this infilling by the heavenly Spirit, our emphasis here is simply that it is a *reality*, and that in answer to the appropriating faith of the fully yielded believer, it is the *first* ingredient in the experience of "entire sanctification".

Its Deeper Effect

Yes, they "were all filled with the Holy Spirit" (Acts 2: 4). They saw, felt, knew, understood, as they never had until that invisible immersion. But there was far more. Those men who were already regenerate were now inwardly *changed*. The records leave no doubt about that. And if we would know more precisely what the change *was*, it is elucidated by the New Testament Epistles in their various comments on the Spirit's deeper work in believers. Not only was there an expansion of spiritual grasp, there was a purifying *renewal* deep in their moral nature. They became radiant incarnations of that resplendent phrase in 1 Timothy 1: 5, "*Love out of a pure heart*".

As it was then, so is it still. Inwrought sanctification is the Holy Spirit's effecting of a penetrating *renewal* in the moral being of the fully yielded Christian. In most cases it is as decidedly distinguishable from *conversion* to Christ as it was in the case of the Apostles—and for clear reasons. Conversion certainly effects a vital change, but *that* change is different from the change which is effected in entire sanctification. At conversion our regeneration was the soul-saving change from spiritual death to new spiritual life. But entire sanctification is a further change in which that new life makes unobstructed penetration to the inmost and deepmost functionings of our thought-life.

Or, to put it another way, at our conversion a wonderful new personal Presence came to be joint-occupier of our personalities along with our now-regenerated human self. But in entire sanctification that heavenly Indweller has been given such utter control that He renews our inner being in all its desires, impulses, thought-springs, motives, tempers and inclinations. Inwrought sanctification is nothing less than that; and oh, it is just as real as it is blessedly wonderful. Those first-century Christians were glowing testimonials to it. There have been glad witnesses to it in every generation since, even in the darkest periods of Christendom. And there are unfaltering voices verifying its equal reality today. This is the spiritual "Canaan" which all in Christ may know! Instead of weary struggles to repress a resiliently evil self with an unconquerable rubbery bounce-back, there is release through renewal, bringing a hitherto unknown inward harmony and a *spontaneous* holiness. Does temptation remain active? Yes, incessantly. Is there a continuing susceptibility to it? Yes, for we are still human, imperfect, deceivable; but the deepest tastes, responses, propensities and reactions of the mind are now so purified that the way of victory is a reigning *over* the "flesh" rather than a fighting it down on its own level.

How is it Attested?

After what we have said it will surprise no one when we add that such an infilling and deep-going renewal is unmistakably *attested* in the consciousness of the Christian believer. Let me quote from a little booklet which a friend gave me over forty years ago. "Will there be *manifestation* of the fullness of the Spirit when we completely yield our lives to Him? Shall we become aware of a great inner change? Will there be a *conscious* new estate of Christian experience? To this we answer: Is the sluggish, stagnant river conscious of the inrushing waters of the sea, as it feels the throb and rush of her cleansing tides? Is the dark, gloomy old castle conscious of the fresh, sweet air that fills its wind-swept chambers, as they are flung wide open to it? Are the sightless eyes, that have been veiled for years in hopeless darkness, conscious of the bright light of day, when it first breaks upon their enraptured vision? So, assuredly, is there a conscious manifestation to the soul that has given itself, for all time and all things, to God. There must be, there will be a change; a realization of His presence to a degree never known before; a consciousness that the greatest crisis in the spiritual life has been passed. Nor does it matter whether such manifestation of His fullness bursts upon us like the sudden outflashing of the sun from behind dark clouds, or steals upon us like the slow-increasing glow of the morning twilight, gradual, but sure. . . . Henceforth there is height and depth, peace and power, joy and blessing, communion and service, prayer and praise, such as the past has never possessed."

To summarize

The Scriptures make clear that this inwrought sanctification is exclusively the work of the Holy Spirit. As 2 Thessalonians 2: 13, says, "God hath from the beginning chosen you to salvation through sanctification of the Spirit". It is something which really occurs within us, not merely some pious fancy dreamily supposed or excitedly imagined. It is a direct divine intervention which strikes deep beneath the upper stratum of the superficial emotions, to the deepmost impulses and motions of our mental and moral being. It makes such a change in the depths that its effects are inevitably seen through the upper and outer expressions of our life, in a purity, simplicity, joyfulness, peacefulness, and resignation never observable before. And this, we repeat, is because such sanctification is the real work of the Holy Spirit within the soul. It is not only consecration on *our* part; it is intervention on *God's* part; it is God's *answer* to the believer's love and faith in becoming a "living sacrifice" to Christ.

Just as in some serious illness, a medical specialist insists that the patient must be committed unreservedly into his hands, so, in this matter of inwrought sanctification, the Lord Jesus, our *Jehovah-Rapha* (the Lord who healeth) insists on our complete and continuous yieldedness. And it is then, when by our own choice we are entirely handed over to Him, that His lovely miracles begin to happen inside us. When once we are thus *fully* His, we may confidently appropriate every promise and provision in His written Word. *Until* we are thus fully His we *cannot* validly "claim" every such promise or provision ; for the deepest, richest experiences of salvation are for the truly consecrated alone, the set-apart-ones, the sanctified. It is to those, and those alone, that Jesus says, "Whatsoever ye shall ask in My name, that will I do". "Ask what ye will, and it shall be done unto you" (John 14: 13; 15: 7). Until we are really *there*—entirely set apart to Christ, the deeper and richer promises of holiness, and the bigger answers to prayers, can no more be ours than the fruitage and bounties of Canaan could be enjoyed by an old-time Israelite living on the wrong side of Jordan.

What new thing, then, is it that the Holy Spirit does, or, rather *begins* to do in those who are fully consecrated? Well, first, He sanctifies or sets apart, from the *divine* side, the soul which has

been sanctified or set apart by voluntary choice on the *human* side.
He begins to give witness of His presence deep in the human consciousness (1 John 5: 10). He begins to make Christ more
luminous and constant to the eyes of the mind (1 John 3: 24;
4: 13). He begins to clarify and expand our apprehension
of spiritual truths (1 Cor. 2: 12, 15). He begins to visit the
soul with fresh enduings of power for service (Luke 24: 49;
Acts 4: 31). He now makes praying a more vivid and meaningful transaction, so that intercession has prevailing power,
and supplication becomes a radiant "fellowship with the Father
and with His Son Jesus Christ" (1 John 1: 3). He now begins to
purify our desires, to refine our tastes, to correct abnormal propensities, to counteract hereditary proclivities, to move us and
elevate us with holy impulses and gracious thoughts from Himself, to "renew" us in the very springs of our being, and to conform our character more decidedly to the "image of Christ", so that
Christ is now "formed within us", and seen more clearly through
us. By a lovely paradox He satisfies all the truest hunger of the soul,
yet at the same time begets an even deeper hunger for more and
more of Christ; so that there is always new hunger and new satis-
faction, and the whole soul flames with the one joyous passion—

Oh, it is time that many more of us were living in this "land of
pure delight", where we "reign in life by One, Jesus Christ"
(Rom. 5: 17). It is time that we crucified our pride, and repented
of our superficiality. "Therefore, also, now saith Jehovah: Turn
ye even to Me with all your heart; with fasting and with weeping
and with mourning; and rend your heart, and not your garments"
(Joel 2: 12). The shining altitudes of sanctification beckon to us.
The first step of ascent is to get *down* in deep and contrite heart-
prostration before the Cross; to have done with mere formalism,
professionalism, triviality, pretence, and sluggish contentedness
with the second-best; and to become utterly overpowered by the
love of Christ into complete surrender to Him. *Then* we may confidently claim and prove the reality of sanctification inwrought
by the Holy Spirit. *Then* it will not be long before we find ourselves singing,

> Oh, this is life! Oh, this is joy!
> My God, to find Thee so!
> Thy face to see; Thy voice to hear;
> And all Thy love to know!

SANCTIFICATION:
ENTIRE AND EFFECTUAL

"I have an exceedingly complex idea of sanctification."

John Wesley (Journal).

"What exactly is sanctification both in its com-
plexity and in its simplicity?"

Alexander Whyte.

"Sanctification is the work of God's free grace
whereby we are renewed in the whole man, after
the image of God."

The Shorter Catechism.

SANCTIFICATION:
ENTIRE AND EFFECTUAL

"A vessel unto honour, sanctified, and meet for the Master's use" (2 Tim. 2: 21).

IN OUR foregoing reflections on personal sanctification, we have considered its imperativeness and practicality, its inward meaning and outward expression, also its crisis and process aspects. In this further adversion to the subject we shall enquire more particularly into its intended *extent,* and its more pronounced *effects,* in the experience of the believer.

As a prelude to this, and gathering up what we have already said, it will be helpful here to fix in mind a kind of pin-point definition of sanctification or, rather, of *entire* sanctification. We have emphasised that in the New Testament use of the word, sanctification has the twofold idea of set-apartness to God, and a resultant purification of the believer's heart and life. We have noted that in it there are two polarities—a negative and a positive; a separation *from sin,* and a separation *to God.* Also, we have observed that there are two sides to it—the human and the divine. The human side is that of a resolute break-free from all wrong in the life over which the will has control, and a whole-hearted self-surrender to God. The divine side is the sealing and ratifying of the believer's self-dedication, by the immediate new operation of the Holy Spirit in the mind and heart and soul, renewing, refining, restoring, infilling as never before, and infusing experiential holiness.

So, then, *entire sanctification is that act and condition in which the believer is gladly and completely separated to God, voluntarily and continually at God's disposal, and therefore unobstructedly infilled and renewed by the Holy Spirit.* Oh, that all of us who are committed followers of our Lord Jesus were living in the experience of such entire sanctification! Then indeed should we "adorn the doctrine of our Saviour-God in all things" (Titus 2: 10).

Now it is noticeable how often the Scriptures insist on this *entire* sanctification. Recall 1 Thessalonians 5: 23, "And the very God of peace sanctify you entirely; and may your whole *spirit* and *soul* and *body* be preserved blameless. . . ." See 1 Peter 1: 15, "But as He which hath called you is holy, so be ye holy in *all manner of behaviour.*" Or turn to 2 Timothy 2: 21, "Sanctified, and meet for the Master's use, and prepared unto *every good work.*" In 2 Corinthians 7: 1, we find this appeal: "Having therefore these promises, dearly beloved, let us cleanse ourselves from *all defilement of flesh and spirit,* fully completing holiness in the fear of God." Or again, mark the exclamation in 2 Peter 3: 11, "What manner of persons ought ye to be in *all holy conduct and godliness!*"

All these and other verses which might be quoted, are the New Testament counterparts of *Old* Testament exhortations to the earthly Israel—from which we may learn much by way of vivid illustration and detail. Not once or twice only, but with solemn reiteration the voice of Jehovah called "out of the tabernacle of the congregation", to the covenant people, "Ye shall be holy, for I, Jehovah your God, am holy" (Lev. 19: 2). "Sanctify yourselves, therefore, and be ye holy; for I, Jehovah, am your God" (20: 7). "Ye shall be holy unto Me; for I, Jehovah, am holy, and have severed you from other people, that ye should be mine" (20: 26).

Nor was that stipulation merely general; it particularized right down to the *details* of life; yes, right down from the "holy crown" of the high priest (Exod. 29: 16), and the strict regulations binding all the other priests (Lev. 21, 22), to the bodies and clothes and foods and habits of every man, woman, and child in each of the twelve tribes (Lev. 18–20). And Moses concentrates all this when he later says, "Jehovah thy God walketh in the midst of thy camp . . . therefore thy camp shall be holy, that He see *NO* unclean thing in thee, and turn away from thee" (Deut. 23: 14).

Alas, the earthly Israel fell foul of the "holy calling", with what centuries of tragic aftermath we all know; but to the end of time, even while "the ordinances of the moon and of the stars" endure, God is graciously self-committed to the unrescindable Abrahamic and Davidic covenants; and when the long historical hiatus of Israel's scattering is over, David's "Greater Son", the Lord Jesus, shall reign gloriously from Jerusalem over a regathered and regenerated Israel. Then, at last, in that culminating millennial restoration, God's holiness ideal for His people shall be realised in every detail of life; for as Zechariah 14: 20 foretells, "In that day shall there be even upon the bridles of the horses, 'Holy unto Jehovah'; and the pots in the Lord's house shall be [holy] as the bowls before the altar. Yea, every pot in Jerusalem and Judah shall be holy unto Jehovah of hosts."

To use a present-day colloquialism, all these quotations "add up" to one conclusion: that God enjoins upon His people a *thoroughgoing* sanctification. If that was true of the earthly Israel long ago, it is even more sacredly so in relation to the *spiritual* Israel, the Church of Christ which He "purchased with His own blood". There can be utterly no relaxation of the high imperative. Our Christian "high calling" cannot under any consideration be accommodated to the moral compromises of the present generation. On the contrary, the slipshod attitudes inside and outside the organized churches today present a desperate new challenge to the Lord's assemblies to hoist high aloft, more resolutely than ever, the true rallying ensign of out-and-out Christian faith: *"HOLI-NESS UNTO THE LORD."*

That, of course, begets some cogent ponderings. According to the text which heads this further examination into our theme, each of us is meant to be "a vessel unto honour, sanctified and meet for the Master's use". That word, "vessel", may well mean the whole human personality, though undoubtedly it has special reference to the *body*, as the immediate context shows. Just as the body was included in the regulations binding those old-time Israelites, so is it included in the gracious calls of the New Covenant to Christian believers. Remember 1 Thessalonians 5: 23, "May your whole spirit and soul and *body* be preserved *blame-less.* . . ." Any thoughtful person is sure to ask how the *body* can be preserved "blameless". The body is the vehicle of the human personality; it provides physical expression to spirit and soul; but the body itself is mere matter; it does not think or decide or act of itself; it is a purely non-moral, non-responsible instrument. To speak of "blame", therefore, as attaching to the body is an irrelevance. Strictly speaking, the body can be neither blameworthy nor blameless. In what sense, then, does Paul speak of the body as "sanctified" and "blameless"?

The first part of the answer is as clear as noonday. We catch the Pauline sense if we insert just one short phrase which, although grammatically absent, is implicitly present in the text:

"May your whole spirit and soul and body, *in all their uses,* be preserved blameless. . . ." Whatever else may or may not be intended, Paul is here thinking mostly of the *uses* to which we put our bodies. It is we ourselves, the persons who live inside these bodies, who are to be "blameless" in every activity of our whole triune being—"spirit and soul and body". It is thus that the body shares in the total sanctification of our humanhood.

This means at once that there must be bodily *discipline.* Appetites, habits, organs, functions, and all other bodily activities over which the will has control, must be held in check suchwise as "becometh godliness". Does this run counter to much modern psychology? That is only because much modern psychology runs contrary to the Word of God. For decades now, prominent psychological teachings have emphasised so-called "self-expression". The child must not be restrained or punished, for such repressions supposedly injure the proper development of personality, and often cause later reactions of dangerous rebellion. The dear little rascal must be allowed to talk or yell as much as he (or she) wants. He (or she) must be able to do just whatever pleases, without any parental thwartings of the imperious little will. When years of puberty are reached, sex desires also must be allowed so-called "normal" expression. What damage to married life, and home life, and social life, and national life such teachings have already brought, no pen could exaggerate. It is endlessly surprising how people can be hoodwinked by catch-titles and sleek slogans. What the psychologists have called "self-expression" is often nothing of the kind; it is the license for *one part only* of human nature to express itself—the lower, the *animal* part! So far as our own observation goes, in seven or eight instances out of ten, when the average psychologist today talks of "self-expression", what he really means is mere *animal* expression. Are there no other parts of our human nature which crave expression? What about the intellectual and moral constituents of human personality which are ever seeking to lift us *above* the merely animal? Must not *these* parts be given expression? Nay, more, just *because* they are the highest and noblest parts, must they not be helped, guided, encouraged, educated?

We gratefully acknowledge all *Christian* psychologists. Psychology in union with Christian truth can make a truly beneficial contribution to human well-being; but with the Bible in our hands we part company from the more secular type of modern psychology and psychiatry. We believe there is a place for parental discipline, and that the lack of it today is a costly farce. Does not a study of human history and autobiography show us the need and the vast profit of cultivating the higher and disciplining the lower? Few mothers could have been stricter than my own—and none more respected or loved. Never can I be too grateful for her disciplines. Never can I thank God enough that the wild young colt named James Sidlow Baxter was firmly but wisely, and sometimes painfully, trained to "bit and bridle". Not long ago, according to a radio newscast, a foreign diplomat visiting America remarked that one of the things which had impressed him most about the average American home was the wonderful *obedience* in it—the obedience of parents to children! The thing would be comic if it were not tragic.

But we have wandered a little, as John Bunyan would say, into a "By-path meadow". We return now to our particular consideration of discipline in relation to sanctification, and we repeat that all appetites, habits, organs and functions of the body over which the will has power must be held in godly control. Paul himself is our exemplar in this. He says, "But I keep under [lit: I buffet] my body, and bring it into subjection . . ." (1 Cor. 9: 27). Paul does not mean that he buffeted his body with *physical* blows. He speaks figuratively, as he also does in the preceding clause where he metaphorically assumes the role of a pugilist—"So do I box, as not smiting the air". Paul was neither fighting with actual fisticuffs nor pummelling his mortal frame with material club or cudgel. By the buffeting of his body he means blows of the will against insubordinate passions, or perverted instincts, or inordinate appetites which the body excites; blows of the will by which the organs and tendencies of the body are overcome, restrained, gradually corrected and regulated. We may all take comfort from the proven fact that the body *can* be thus disciplined and successfully rendered subservient to the higher impulses of the mind. This is even truer of those who through conversion to Christ have the new life of regeneration within them, for this new life brings with it its own heavenward impulses and its powerful repulsion of those grosser inclinations which Paul calls "the flesh".

Let it be understood clearly and finally that by discipline of the body and its members we do not mean any kind of *punishing* the body by morbid monastic thrashings or ascetic rigours or fanatical starvings. Real discipline is Scriptural, healthful and wholesome; but its monastic caricatures are unscriptural, misguided and injurious. Nor is this discipline any kind of *disfiguring* the body, after the manner of India's "holy men" and others. All such religious penalising or disfiguring of the body springs from the old Gnostic notion that matter itself is evil, and that the human body is therefore sinful in itself. Christianity came to do away with that falsehood once for all. The very Son of God "became flesh", conjoining to Himself a real human body through which to glorify God; and now the bodies of all the redeemed in Christ are sanctuaries of the divine Spirit. "Know ye not that your body is a temple of the Holy Spirit within you, which ye have from God? And ye are not your own; for ye were bought with a price; glorify God therefore in your *body*" (I Cor. 6: 19, 20, E.R.V.).

Sanctification of the body means the resolute preservation of it from all forms of *over-indulgence*, whether in eating and drinking, or in marital function, or in health-weakening business-absorption, or in idle indoor lazing. It means abstention from all habits unchaste or unclean or provenly harmful, which, to our own thinking, clearly proscribes tobacco-smoking, non-medical drugs, and alcoholic beverages. We do not presume to dictate; yet neither can we stifle our sincere conviction that such indulgences are incompatible with the entire sanctification to which God calls us.

Sanctification of the body, however, besides these interdictive aspects, has its positive side. The body is to be given thoughtful *care*—the more so inasmuch as it is now a "temple of the Holy Spirit" and thus indeed sacred. Bodily sanctification surely means care concerning the foods we eat, and the liquids we drink, and the air we breathe. In these present days, especially in intricately organised countries like America and Britain, food and drink and air become a problem such as they never used to be. What with processed cereals, canned vegetables, bleached flour, refined and whitened sugar, preservative-injected meats and patent foods, artificial chemical fertilizers in fields and groves, fluorinated drinking-water in our cities, dried, pickled, or otherwise (often) devitalised foods, and all kinds of more-or-less harmful chemical preservatives in the eating commodities which we buy from the grocery stores, the problem of getting fresh, unadulterated, still-vital and nutritious foods becomes increasingly real. I am neither a finical gourmet nor an abstemious food-crank; I am neither a physician nor a nutritionist; but as a Christian I have some quite decided views about certain matters pertaining to human physiology. I believe that *preventing* disease is far better than trying to cure it after it has come. I believe that the best resistance to disease is a full measure of vitality derived from healthful habits of life, and a really natural, nutritious diet. I believe that the body falls prey to destructive parasitic bacteria only when it has become more or less weakened, toxic, degenerative, through vitiating habits or adulterated and devitalized foods. Clinical experiments have demonstrated that pathogenic bacteria cannot beget their characteristic diseases in a normal organism possessing the full vitality which comes of really natural or scientific living. Those evil parasitic or saprophytic micro-organisms called bacteria, or germs, or microbes, which cause disease in human bodies are opportunists. They swoop and breed only where they find the toxic condition or "culture" medium on which they thrive. The body which is treated, exercised and fed in accord with Nature's simple but adamant requirements always finds that the best bulwark against infection is robust health. Nutritional foods, healthful ways of living, and a resultant top-standard vitality, are Nature's ramparts of immunity to disease. Experiments have proved beyond any peradventure that deficiency in proteins, various vitamins and minerals predisposes the body to corresponding ailments.

I sometimes wonder whether our over-complex and hyper-commercialised "civilisation" in America and Britain is now beginning to produce a cancer-prone race. I am no fanatical alarmist, but I think it is time a "hue and cry" was raised against the racket in exaggeratedly advertised but inferior, artificial, processed, and preservative-dosed "foods". Especially in America, is there not far too much eating in cafés and restaurants instead of at home? Often the penalty paid in consuming bulk rather than true food is very high. I agree in general with the advice, "Keep off white bread and white sugar", the whitening is harmful. I agree, also, with a comment in a recent diet book that the continually indulged "white-toast-and-strong-tea-or-coffee-habit" can eventually prove as harmful as tobacco or even whiskey. To this I would add: Beware of over-eating. Gluttony and sanctity are incompatible with each other. Far better eat a little too little than much too much. Over-eating is a sin against the body; it is an enemy of health, and often causes serious sickness. Far too many early graves are digged with knives and forks.

As far as possible we should see to it that the foods we buy are guaranteed pure and free from harmful preservatives. We should guard against over-consumption of flesh meat, especially along with an under-supply of fresh vegetables and greens. I am not a vegetarian, but I think that in general there is too much flesh eaten today in proportion to the rest of our diet. It is a notable fact that the strongest of all the wild animals, the gorilla, is not carnivorous, but herbivorous. The strongest of all the semi-tameable animals, the elephant, is not carnivorous, but herbivorous. The strongest of all the amphibians, the hippopotamus, is not carnivorous, but herbivorous. The strongest of all the tamed animals, the horse, is not carnivorous, but herbivorous. And, as a rule, even the animals which *are* carnivorous, or flesh-eaters, will eat only the flesh of animals which are *non*-meat-eaters. Those facts may well speak to us.

As always, the Bible is our sanest guide. We find that in the beginning man's food was to be the produce of the earth (Gen. 1: 29). Later, meat was included (Gen. 9: 3), and its use confirmed under the Mosaic economy, but only with most definite restrictions (Lev. 11: 1–47, and 17: 13–15). Many people today, I believe, would benefit by taking rather less meat, far more fresh vegetables, and more raw fruits. However, it is not my intention to pose as a diet specialist, so I will venture no further philosophizings on foods. What I *will* suggest is that it would at least be wise for all Christian believers to get some expert guidance on modern foods and on the kind of diet which makes for good health. I rather shrink from suggesting by name books which give guidance on health diet, for there are always some readers who easily get exaggerated ideas and become food cranks —which is one of the *worst* things for health. However, I will risk recommending *two* books which I consider in the main to give sound, expert guidance. Indeed, it would be good for many a person's physical health to read again the dietary sanctions of the Mosaic economy, with its "No blood" and "No fat" prohibitions (Lev. 7: 23, 24, 26, 27), and other regulations from the Greatest of all food authorities. We shall have more to say about this in a later chapter on "Sanctification and the Law". Meanwhile, I recommend the following two books: (1) *Let's Eat Right to Keep Fit,* by Dr. Adelle Davis, A.B., M.S., and (2) *The Wheel of Health,* by G. T. Wrench, M.D.

The body should be given plenty of fresh air. Oxygen is vital to it. It should be given regular exercise as best befits our time of life. We should practise deep breathing, and adhere to hygienic habits. We should avoid drugs of every kind, except in serious health crises, and even then only under strict, expert supervision. But while the body should be nourished and cared for, it should never be coddled. Our care of it should be with a view to hardiness; coddling tends to invalidism. All these remarks, however, are meant for those whose health is normal. There are those, as we only too sympathetically realise, whose condition requires that health be nursed. Such ill-health does not lessen, but rather increases, the importance of bodily sanctification; for real sanctification gives the Holy Spirit opportunity to quicken the body and quieten the mind as only He can.

Another aspect of the matter is how we *clothe* the body. Some people seem to think that in this connection sanctification is synonymous with slovenliness or even outlandishness; but they are wrong. For the truth's sake we should dress normally and becomingly, in reasonable accord with accepted modes. Real sanctification never makes dowdies or oddities. The old-time Pharisees confused sanctification with *sanctimoniousness.* They adopted a religiosity of raiment and adornment, with wide skirt-borders and demonstrative phylacteries, or, at other times, austerity-apparel to indicate pious fasting. Our Lord rebuked it all. In contrast, He said, "When thou fastest, anoint thine head, and wash thy face". So real sanctity of heart has its proper counterpart in a well-groomed head.

The clothes we Christians wear should be clean, tidy, up-to-date, and of as good quality as we can comfortably afford. It is not wrong to pay attention to personal appearance; it is wrong *not* to pay attention to it. Yet as soon as self-respecting normality becomes showy pride of apparel we indulge vanity, which is sin. Vanity cannot be sanctified; it must be crucified.

This has an underscored relevance to *feminine* attire. Our Christian womenfolk, both the younger and the older, are needing to rediscover today, that they can be *à la mode* without exorbitant finery or loud self-exhibition. The way a woman dresses can beget for her an immediate gentlemanly respect—or the opposite. Many of the older women have learned at last, and all the younger

women should learn at once, that no woman is ever really loved
who is not really respected, however much she may for a time stir
the animal passions of the male sex by bizarre cut-aways or
figure-emphasising ensemble.

In an earlier address we compared our tripartite human constitution to the old Israelite tabernacle—"outer court" the body,
"holy place" the soul, "holy of holies" the spirit. We noted also
that the materials used for the outer court were inferior to those
used for the two main parts of the inner sanctuary. How this
speaks to us in the matter of clothes and other bodily adornments!
If most of us spent a quarter of the time in prayer that we expend
even on *extras* for the body, what saints we should be! Yet the
body, the "outer court", is the least important part of the human
"tabernacle". Again and again at seaside resorts I have wished
that the women would wear a few more "hangings" round the
outer court!—which leads to a further remark, namely, that if
some of our sparsely clad females would realise how difficult they
make it for many men not to think wrong thoughts, they would
be more considerate. Some of the sincerest younger men I have
ever met have confided to me the temptations often occasioned
to them through immodest feminine attire—or lack of it. You
younger Christian women, lay it well to heart: sanctification and
immodest fashions cannot live together.

Then, too, what about the use of *cosmetics*? Never was there
a former generation to compare with ours in face-figure-and-foot
artistry. Who in the Church shall set himself up to judge and
dictate? Christian liberty in all such matters is a heritage far too
precious to violate. There is a proper use for a hair oil or a
shampoo. So there is for a face cream or powder. There is no more
wrong in seeking to improve one's appearance than there is in
seeking to increase one's proficiency in a game, or to foster one's
usefulness in conversation. Some of the pious elderly are far more
prone to reprimand and interdict than they are to understand,
or to recall their own bygone days of youthful début.

The fact is, that here, as in other connections, there is a kind
of invisible line which determines rightness or wrongness. In art,
in literature, in humour, in dress, there is a subtle line, not
always easily detectable, but always "sensed", beyond which the
genuinely aesthetic degenerates into veneered rudeness. Yes, we
agree, there is a permissible use of certain cosmetics, but when it
comes to ultra-red lips, flaming complexion, plucked and substi-

tuted eyebrows, bleached or dyed hair, painted nails (or feminine talons as they often deserve to be called) then, so it seems to me, the commendable has degenerated into the condemnable; the virtuous has given place to the vulgar; liberty has been treated as licence; and the flashy artificiality advertises a worldly spirit behind the cosmetic artistry.

What applies to clothes and cosmetics also applies to *jewelry*. Moreover, lest in saying this we seem to be voicing merely our own private views, it is good to consult the pronouncements of Scripture. In I Timothy 2: 9, 10, we find: "In like manner also, that the women adorn themselves in seemly apparel, with modesty and discreetness; not with plaitings, or gold, or pearls, or costly clothes; but (what is becoming to women professing godliness) with good works." I Peter 3: 3, 4, adds, "Whose adorning let it not be the outward broidering of hair, and wearing around of gold, or putting on of fine raiment; but in the hidden being of the heart, in that which is not corruptible, even a meek and quiet spirit, which is of great price in *God's* sight".

Anyone who knows how garish and excessive the adornments of old-time eastern women were, especially those of a certain social type, will know at once that these words of Paul and Peter were a protest against extravagance, rather than a total prohibition. It was no purpose of theirs to inaugurate a brand of strait-laced "plain Janes". Their meaning is that the *strong emphasis* is to be put on the inward and spiritual; *not* on the outward and worldly.

To sum up, then: by sanctification of the body we mean its blameless use and proper discipline; its nourishment by the most healthful foods which circumstances allow; its preservation from unclean or weakening indulgences; its conservation by hygienic habits, adequate fresh air, sleep, and exercise; its dissociation from all dishonest or otherwise unworthy employment; and its attire in cleanly, normal, attractive but modest adornment.

Thus, sanctification of the body involves continuing consecration and resolution on the part of the Christian believer; but, oh, what *rewards* it brings! When the body is thus sanctified, then it becomes, not merely virtually, but *verily* a "temple of the Holy Spirit". Then the Holy Spirit begins to augment and sublimate our honouring of the sacred vessel. He quickens the brain, and quietens the nerves. He rests the body in easier slumber, and strengthens it for daily challenges.

Observation leads me to aver that most of us who suffer from rasped nerves, indigestive upsets, flops of depression, lowered blood-counts, recurrent functional disorders, palpitation, slumps of lassitude, and other such ailments, would soon find far more relief, or actual cure, by being sanctified, "spirit and soul and *body*", than from all the drugs in the drug-stores. Indeed, a chemist himself recently remarked to me, "I make my living mostly by selling commodities which I would never take myself, and which most of my buyers would find needless if they lived hygienically"!

I am not roving in the realms of pleasant imagination merely when I add that the best of all cosmetics is this sanctification of "spirit and soul and *body*". The unhindered Holy Spirit transfusing the life and love of Christ within the heart, and gently pervading the human personality, gradually imparts, even to the face, a mellow beauty compared with which the lipstick-rouge-and-hair-dye variety is paltry and pathetic. May I slightly reword a chorus we sometimes sing? —

> Let the beauty of Jesus be seen in me,
> All His wonderful likeness reflected be:
> Come, O Spirit divine,
> All my nature refine,
> Till the beauty of Jesus is seen in me.

Well, without exaggeration, that is the lovely, inward metamorphosis which gradually develops when we are really sanctified. Nor is it only inward; for that which is inward soon begins to show through the outward. It begins to transmit itself through looks and tones, through features and expression, in quieter nerves, and calmer reactions, and steadier health, and more genial disposition. The body becomes a "vessel unto honour". The very face gradually catches and holds and emits the gentle glow and beauty of the indwelling Shekinah.

Some elderly or aged friend may be wistfully soliloquising, "Ah, me; youth and bloom have fled; Spring has given place to Autumn; verve and alacrity are no more; how can such beauty belong any more to *this* decrepit old frame?" Our reply is: Dear elderly friend, even the superbest gaiety of the Spring cannot outrival the mellow, golden loveliness of the Autumn. Indeed, ambitious Spring has no meaning without the harvest glories of the Autumn. Never forget that Spring was *made* for Autumn.

Nature expends her ripest artistries upon Autumn. It is even so with youth versus age. There is a beauty in age which youth cannot surpass. The glorious, leaf-decked, full-grown tree never need envy the young uncertain sapling. I say it with utter genuineness: the most beautiful faces I have ever seen on earth were those, not of young, but of elderly people, of dear old saints who had lived the sanctified life, and whose faces were already reflecting the shinings of the heavenly city to which they were soon going. When tourists rove around the British Isles or over the European mainland, what is it that they most wish to see? Is it the giant modern buildings which are the pride of twentieth century engineering, but which in most instances are bleakly devoid of elegance? No; it is the tottery old abbeys, the glorious old cathedrals, the picturesque old cottages, still standing only because of props and stays, but made sacred by great souls who lived in them. These buildings have a glory and sanctity and appeal which only age can give. Dear old saints, take note of this!

There was once an old sculptor who had, among other choice pieces of work in his workshop, the model of a beautiful cathedral. Yet although it was an exquisitely finished miniature replica, nobody admired it as it lay there, covered with the dust of years. One day, however, he engaged a new attendant, who, as he dusted round, placed a light inside the model, whereupon the gleams shone through the beautiful stained glass windows, giving a wonderful new beauty to the whole thing; and all who now came near, stopped to admire it. The entire transformation was wrought by the shining out of the new light within. That, without any exaggeration, is a parable of what begins to happen in and through our human personalities when we become really and entirely sanctified—"spirit and soul and *body*".

> More of Thy glory let me see,
> Thou Holy, Wise, and True;
> I would Thy living image be,
> In joy, in sorrow too.
>
> Fill me with gladness from above,
> Hold me by strength divine;
> Lord, let the glow of Thy great love
> Through my whole being shine.

SANCTIFICATION:
THE GOAL OF ELECTION

"To one who thought that we needed a little sin in our hearts to keep us *humble,* we ventured to reply: 'Then why not have a great deal and be *perfectly* humble?' . . . Just as a child with an organic disease grows slowly and unevenly, if at all, so a Christian who has not become entirely sanctified grows very irregularly. There must be *health* before there can be real and vigorous *growth.*"

Thomas Cook.

"Between God and sin there can be no compromise; and all talk about 'visitations' of evil which have a half-beneficent ministry is a dreadful ignoring both of its deadly nature and also of the fact that it never just 'visits', it stains and stays."

William E. Sangster.

SANCTIFICATION:
THE GOAL OF ELECTION

"According as He hath chosen us in Him before the foundation of the world, that we should be holy and without blame before Him in love" (Eph. 1: 4).

WITH such texts as this in the New Testament, we must surely say again that if there is one thing more than another about which we Christian believers ought to be continually concerned, it is our personal holiness of heart and life. If you and I are among the Lord's redeemed, we do well to call a halt at Ephesians 1: 4, compelling the mind deliberately to "encounter" it. We ought to read it slowly and reflectively, letting every word make its due impact. If we do so, we soon begin to realise how startling, how staggering, how stupendous it is: *"He [God] hath chosen us in Him [Christ] before the foundation of the world, that we should be holy and without blame before Him, in love."*

The perpetual surprise of the verse is its disclosure that our present and future holiness is the underlying purpose of a *premundane divine election*. Before the first sunrise gilded the pristine loveliness of Eden; before our earth flung up its rugged mountain ramparts; before the hemispheres first wove their tropic or arctic tapestries; before primordial chaos became defined into newly organised cosmos; before Orion and Pleiades flashed their flaming effulgence into stellar vasts; God fore-chose us, in Christ, with this in view, *"that we should be holy and without blame before Him in love"*! Either this is the most fantastic fairy-tale ever foisted on credulous minds, or it is the most astounding truth ever unveiled. We believe it to be the latter, for it comes to us in the Book which bears throughout its pages the unmistakable credentials and imprimatur of the universe's King.

This mystery of our pre-cosmic election in Christ may be baffling to the intellect, but it is sunshine to the heart. Should it not also be powerfully salutary to the *conscience*? Divine election, although it is sovereignly arbitrary, is never capricious or indulgent. It is always motivated by ethical purpose. Its very "ethos" is moral, reflecting the utter holiness of God Himself. The first objective of election is not our creature happiness, but our moral *holiness*. The conditioning purpose is that we should be sanctified; the consummating purpose is that the sanctified shall be glorified. Does not this sheer mystery of pre-terrestrial election provoke awed pondering within us? Does not this election with a view to our sanctification stir us into concern to be what the electing Deity purposed, namely, *"hcly and without blame before Him in love"*? If not, we have ample reason to doubt whether we are even among the fore-chosen. I am persuaded, however, that many of us are earnestly and reverently bent on "completing holiness in the fear of God" (2 Cor. 7: 1). Many of us can truly say,

> How I long to fulfil
> The design of His will
> Who chose me ere time had begun,
> Predetermining me
> By election to be
> In the mystical bride of His Son!

So, then, let us look observantly into our text: "According as He hath chosen us in Him [Christ] before the foundation of the world, that we should be holy, and without blame before Him in love." Pause first at the one and only *verb* in the text: *"He hath chosen"*—one word only in the Greek (the pronoun, "He", being implicit in the verb). As the planets of our solar system rotate round the sun, so, in this text, all else revolves around this central verb, "He hath chosen". The rest of the verse consists of adverbial amplification. Thus, if we ask *how* God chose us, the first adverbial phrase answers, "In Him" (Christ). If we ask *when* God chose us, the second adverbial phrase answers, "Before the foundation of the world". If we ask *why* God chose us, the third adverbial amplification answers, "That we should be holy and without blame before Him, in love". Here, then, we have the "how", "when", "why", of divine election.

This verb is a world in a word. Let me here mention three signal features. First, in the Greek it is in the *aorist* tense, which has no exact equivalent in our English grammar of the verb. The Greek aorist denotes an action considered as a whole, and in the past. In the case of an event, it means past and complete. In the case of a transaction it means past and over with. It is often said to mean "once-for-all", which, however, is a reading into it rather more than its strict grammatical sense allows, though it often *acquires* that additional force when taken with its context. For instance, in the English sentence, "His doctor eventually found the trouble, and removed it", we naturally assume, unless informed otherwise, that the trouble was "removed" *permanently*. Similarly, the aorist tense of the verb in our text, inasmuch as it denotes a completed act before the very foundation of the world, certainly carries with it the idea of an eternal finality. Yes, in this case, that aorist *does* signify "once for all", indicating the perpetuity of the divine decree and the everlasting security of the saints.

Do I address some doubting Thomas? You really *are* trusting Christ as Saviour; you would never dream of trusting anyone or anything other than that dear Sin-bearer and His Cross of atonement; yet you do not have the *assurance* of salvation. Let me point you to that aorist tense in Ephesians 1: 4. It says that before ever human history began, you were elected of God in one completed divine act, that is, you were elected once for all. It means that God will never give you up, and never let you go. Get your eye on that God-given guarantee! What solid rock on which to find firm standing! What a comforting pillow on which to rest your heart!

But second, the verb is also in the *middle voice*. Someone uninitiated into the happy mysteries of Greek is sure to ask, "What on earth is the 'middle voice'?" At the risk of sounding facetious let me reply that the "middle voice" is the one which comes between the other two! Yes, that is it: in a way, it comes between the active and the passive, and blends them. In the active voice of the verb, the subject *does* something through the verb to the object. In the passive voice, the subject *sustains* something through the verb from the predicate. In the Greek "middle" voice, the verb goes out from the subject to the object, as in the active voice, but with a kind of boomerang effect it swings back on the subject again. In our text the effect is: "He hath chosen us" (in which the subject, "He", goes out actively through the verb, "hath chosen", to the object, "us"); but then it swings right back to the subject again, in the implied sense of "He hath chosen us *for Himself*", or "to be His own possession". Weymouth's translation captures the sense for us: "He chose us to be *His own* in Christ. . . ." This at once indicates that in divine election there is both the outreach and the embrace of gracious fatherly love and magnanimity. He chose us to be a peculiar treasure to Himself.

In a larger and lovelier sense it parallels with Psalm 135: 4, "Jehovah hath *chosen* Jacob unto *Himself*, even Israel to be His *peculiar treasure*". What deep and tender father-love it expresses!

Third, the verb is compound, or, more explicitly, it has the preposition *ex*, prefixed to it. That little prefix *ex*, always has the connotation, "out of", as in many of our English words such as "exit" (which, of course, is the Latin third person singular verb, "he goes *out of*") and "excavate", meaning to "hollow *out of*". Here, in Ephesians 1: 4, God has *ex*-chosen us, or chosen us *out of*. At once we touch depthless mystery; for this undoubtedly implies an elect minority as distinct from a non-elect majority. Let us at once "give the lie" to that hyper-Calvinism which dares to say that God predestinates millions of His creatures to eternal damnation. Never has a more monstrous libel been cast upon the holy Creator. Evolutionary fatalism or even outright atheism is preferable to *that!* It turns the divine sovereignty into a terrible despotism. The Bible nowhere comes within measurable distance of any such idea. Romans 9 and 10 and 11, those chapters which have been the "happy hunting ground" for hyper-Calvinists, have been murderously misinterpreted because of failure to appreciate their *scope* in the total structure of the epistle. They discuss God's dealings with men and nations historically and dispensationally; they do *not* expound individual salvation and destiny *beyond the grave*. Calvinism is wrong when it reads into problem verses like those of chapter 9: 14–22 election either to salvation or to damnation in the eternal sense. That is not their scope. They belong only to a divine economy of *history*. Paul opens the paragraph by asking, "Is there unrighteousness with God?"—and the rest of the paragraph is meant to show that the answer is "No". If, however, those verses referred to *eternal* life and death, there *would* be unrighteousness with God; and that which is implanted deepest in our moral nature by God Himself would cry out in protest that even God has no *honourable* right to create human beings whose destiny, in millions upon millions, is a predetermined, never-ending Gehenna.

One thing which has always seemed passing strange to my own mind in the Calvinism-versus-Arminianism controversy, is the seeming oversight that election, in the *eternal* sense (as distinct from the corporate or national election of Israel) has especially to do with inclusion in the *Ecclesia*, that is, in the mystic body and bride and temple of God's dear Son. God, who foreknows to the end of time all the "Yes" and "No" reactions of the human will to truth, has superimposed upon human history (without violating the royalty of any human will) a pre-decree that independently of the final, aggregate human response, there shall be an elect *ecclesia* of called-out-ones, who shall be brought into such sublimely sacred union with His Redeemer-Son that the only metaphors approximating to it are those of Head and body, Bridegroom and bride, Foundation and building; that is, the closest possible union of *life,* the tenderest possible union of *love,* and the strongest possible expression of *indissolubility.*

So far as all other human beings are concerned, the Bible nowhere says that they are all going to eternal doom by wholesale consignment. It says that at death they pass as disembodied human beings into Hades, to await the final, general *judgment* of our race at the Great White Throne. At that vast, solemn, final Assize, cases will be tried, evidences weighed, verdicts reached, sentences passed, and destinies decided, by the one Judge who is the infallible Psychologist, the omniscient Examiner, and the inerrant Arbiter. It will go fearfully with the finally impenitent, for the Judge is the Creator-Father—and the anger of a father is far more terrible than the anger of a judge; and the "wrath of the Lamb" is far more terrible than that of the "roaring lion"! But it will be a *judgment*; a judgment of absolute, inflexible, irreversible *righteousness*; and therefore it will *not* be a wholesale consignment to the "lake of fire".

Why do theologians not recognise that the elect "Ecclesia" and the "damnation of Gehenna" are not unaccompanied *alternatives?* The Bible itself does not teach that it is "either—or" between membership in the mystic "body" and damnation in Gehenna. Will there be no *intermediate* levels of being? No blood-bought, born-again, Christian believer will stand before the Great White Throne, for the Calvary Sinbearer bore all the believer's sin-penalty. Therefore, all those who stand before that awesome tribunal will be other than regenerated Christian believers. But does the Word say that all those arraigned millions go indiscriminately to the "lake of fire"? Let him prove it from the Bible who can. The *Biblical* description of that overwhelming scene surely denotes otherwise. Revelation 20: 15 indicates that the "book of life" cannot be restricted either to the Ecclesia or only to the Christian dispensation; and at the same time it shows that not all of that immense multitude go to eternal fire. Must there not be degrees of punishment, if the judgment is a *real* judgment? Will there be no discrimination between a vile Nero or a blood-reeking Stalin and a noble Socrates or other such non-Christian seeker after God? Are all the Old Testament godly included in the New Testament *ecclesia*? My own view is that they are not; yet I am just as certain that they are *"saved"* from eternal ruin through the interposition of Calvary.

Let no one think that what we are saying is even a step in the direction of "universalism", or that it gives the smallest loophole to the Christ-rejector. Nay, it underlines the irreversible doom of the finally lost, and it draws the line between the believer and the *un*believer more vividly than ever. The Word of God says that there is one class of human beings who are condemned before ever they stand at the Great White Throne, namely, those who know the redeeming love of God in Christ but spurn it. Such Christ-rejectors are not merely neutral *non*-believers, like millions of the heathen who have never even heard the name of Jesus; they are *un*believers, and the Word says, concerning them, "He that believeth not is judged [or sentenced] already, because he hath not believed in the name of the only-begotten Son of God" (John 3: 18). Far better to have been born into the crass ignorance of stark heathenism, and never have heard a syllable of the Gospel, than to know it and reject it, and thus seal one's doom for ever!

Paul the apostle was acutely sensitive to this heightening of responsibility which results from hearing the Gospel. It was with fervent awe that he wrote, "To the one we are the savour of death unto death; and to the other the savour of life unto life, and who is sufficient for these things?" (2 Cor. 2: 16). All will be judged. All sin will be punished. There is no loophole. It will go fearfully for the wicked. The lake of fire is the extreme penalty, but it is not the *only* penalty. There *must* be degrees of punishment for degrees of guilt, even as there are degrees of reward for godly faithfulness and service. We are tempted to go further into this, but we forbear, as it would not be really germane to our present subject. We have said this much in order that we may see this matter of election to sanctification in its big and solemn relationships to eternal destiny, and to the transcendent wonder of inclusion in the *Ecclesia* of the called-out-ones who compose the mystic body and bride and temple of the Eternal Son.

Tremendous as is the wonder of our salvation in its negative sense (our everlasting rescue from the "outer darkness" and the "second death" and Gehenna flame in the endless Beyond) the supreme marvel is not what we are saved *from,* but what we are saved *to.* Although we are hereditarily corrupt, and by nature "children of wrath", and sinners by a million rebellious transgressions of the moral law, and inexcusably guilty, and deservedly exposed to banishment from the divine presence; yet having been washed from our damning guilt in the "precious blood" of Christ, the Lamb of God; having been regenerated into new spiritual life and Godward sonship; having been renewed and sanctified, and made members of the mystic bride of Christ, we are to be lifted up, in the ultimate consummation, above angels and principalities and powers, and above all other ranks of intelligences in the realm beyond—yes (so it would seem) even above the very cherubs and flaming seraphs, in that closest of all love-unions with God's dear Son which can only be expressed by the startling metaphor of Bridegroom and bride. What that mysterious union and inconceivable sublimation will yet mean for us, only the unfolding ages of eternity will reveal. *That* is the supreme wonder of our salvation in Christ! That is what was foreinvolved in the divine "out-choosing" of us "before the foundation of the world"! Oh, the all-eclipsing wonder, that *we* were chosen, then called, converted, regenerated, and thus included in the *Ecclesia,* the "body", the "temple", the "bride"! How can we but be everlastingly "lost in wonder, love and praise"?

Away back in the Victorian days, when Spurgeon and Parker and Liddon were reigning in their London pulpits, a sceptical wag accosted Joseph Parker with the poser, "If Jesus Christ knew everything, as you say He did, why did He choose Judas who betrayed Him?" Parker hesitated, then with deep emotion replied, "Man, I have a bigger problem than that: why did Jesus choose *me?*" Is not that how many of us feel and wonder? "Why did Jesus choose *me?*" Eternity alone will disclose the full answer, but meanwhile, here is one big part of it: "He chose us . . . that we should be *holy and without blame before Him, in love.*"

Look back again over those three features of that verb, "He hath chosen": aorist tense—completedly for ever; middle voice—"for His own possession": *ex*-chosen—to be a separated people. Do not such considerations bring us to our knees in heart-searching prayer and deep longing to be what God *elected* us to be, even "holy and without blame before Him, in love"?

Look back again, also, over those adverbial phrases. The first of them says that God chose us *"in Him"* (Christ). We were chosen, not because we *were* holy, but in order to *become* holy. Therefore, since it is impossible for us to make ourselves holy, the means of holiness must be divinely provided. Christ is the provision. Holiness is not an achievement through self-struggle, but an inwrought transmorphosis which becomes ours in Christ, through self-surrender and receptive faith.

The second adverbial phrase adds that God elected us in Christ *"before the foundation of the world"*. If then, our election to holiness has proceeded from those impenetrable depths of eternity, is it likely that the purpose of God has veered round somewhat during the last sixty years? To hear certain modern preachers one might think so. They seem to read the text, "God hath chosen us . . . to be social workers, or educators, or religious organizers". Such is the educated blindness of the hour! But the ages-long purpose of God is inflexible. His undeviating first requirement in us, His people, is *holiness*.

The third adverbial amplification brings us right to the heart of our subject: "That we should be *holy*. . . ." What, then, *is* holiness? That is the crucial question. Does our text indicate the kind of holiness required, and the way into it? I think it does. Reflect carefully on the wording here: "That we should be holy *and* . . ." Even the little copula, "and", is meaningful here. It represents the Greek conjunction, *kai*, which, although usually having the sense of "and", is sometimes rendered as "also", or "but", or "even", not to mention other English equivalents. In over one hundred instances our King James Version renders it by the word, *"even"*. That is its sense in our text: "He hath chosen us . . . that we should be holy, even [or, which equals] *without blame* before Him, in love." We need not unduly press this, but it certainly helps to clarify the meaning. Consider this carefully: "holy" here equals *"without blame"*.

Indeed, that is both crux and focus. The holiness to which God calls us here on earth, at present, is not faultlessness, but *blamelessness*. We have mentioned this in an earlier study; but now let us look into it more particularly. It is a point at which many of those who misunderstand holiness go wrong; therefore we should fix it the more firmly in our minds. It is not merely propositional—something to be believed, doubted, or denied; it is categorical:

THE SANCTIFICATION OR HOLINESS TO WHICH THE NEW TESTAMENT CALLS US IN THIS PRESENT LIFE IS NOT FAULTLESSNESS BUT BLAMELESSNESS.

The sharp and vital difference between faultlessness and blamelessness, as already remarked, is that faultlessness has to do with our natural powers or *faculties*, whereas blamelessness has to do with our inner moral activity, especially our *motives*. It is well to get this permanently fixed in our minds: faultlessness has to do with our *faculties*; blamelessness has to do with our *motives*.

In this present life we shall never have faultlessness of our natural faculties. The "infirmities of the flesh" and the other impediments of our fallen nature will cling around us until "this mortal shall have put on immortality". These, however, do not preclude the possibility of real holiness in the sense of *blamelessness*. A sanctified man may make many mistakes, but mistakes are not sins; nor is an error of judgment the breaking of a commandment. A right action with a wrong motive is a sin, for even a kiss can be the act of a Judas; but an unintendedly wrong action with a pure motive is no sin; it is a blunder.

A little boy thought to give his tired and busy daddy a pleasant surprise by cleaning up the garden. With busy hands he did swift and drastic work, pulling out not only weeds but chrysanthemum roots, flower seedlings, tulip bulbs, and what not! When daddy returned the surprise was bigger than sonny had intended. The flower-beds were wonderfully tidy—and ruined. The wee laddie had made a most unfortunate mistake; but would even the dismayed father say that he had committed a *sin*? Nay, for the motive was pure as could be. I remember reading somewhere about a little girl in Lancashire, England, who, knowing that her mother had to go out one wintry night, thoughtfully put her mother's shoes in the oven to warm (it was in the days when most living-room fireplaces in English cottages had a cooking oven adjoining the fireplace). The oven was quite hot, and, of course, the shoes were roasted beyond repair. The well-meaning little mite had made a costly mistake; but had she committed a *sin*? No, for the motive was lovely. Sin always has to do with *motive*.

Some of the holiest Christian men I have ever met have had notoriously bad memories; and some of the saintliest Christian women have been all too gullible in matters of natural judgment; but a bad memory is not a sin, it is a tiresome nuisance; and a gullible judgment is not a sin, but an unfortunate disability. Infirmities are not iniquities; gout is not guilt; disabilities are not culpabilities. No judge or magistrate ever pronounced a man guilty of deafness or a bad cough! Nor does any law of God hold a man guilty either for hereditary incapabilities or mistakes arising therefrom. That which brings guilt or moral blame always has to do with *motive*.

Even in this present life, thank God, the Gospel makes interim provision for Christian believers over against such natural disabilities. Although, in this present dispensation, our human nature is not restored to its Edenic perfection, the Gospel answers such infirmities as bad memory and erring judgment by the wonderful ministry of the Holy Spirit as the ever-abiding *Paraclete*. Over against my ailing memory, the Word says, "He shall bring to your remembrance . . ." (John 14: 26). Over against my defective judgment, the promise is, "And He shall guide you into all the truth" (John 16: 13). Indeed, the Paraclete ministry of the Spirit is specifically adapted to such requirements of the Lord's people in their present condition on earth. He is the "Spirit of wisdom and revelation" who enlightens "the eyes of our understanding" (Eph. 1: 17, 18), and "quickens" all our natural faculties, as is so graphically represented to us in the Acts of the Apostles. This precious aspect of the matter, however, we mention only incidentally here.

Returning to our reflections on natural infirmities in relation to holiness, let us gratefully re-emphasize the point that our lamented "infirmities of the flesh and of the mind" do not preclude the possibility of real holiness, since holiness, being a *moral* quality, has to do with motive. A man who goes down with smallpox may afterwards bear the pockmarks as long as he lives; yet although the pockmarks persist, the disease which caused them may be cleared from his system. A man may be shot in the arm, with a poisoned bullet, and the arm for ever afterwards may have only a subnormal mobility; yet although the arm is thus impaired, both bullet and poison may have been thoroughly extracted from it, so that the arm is poisoned no more. There are diseases like polio, which leave certain organs of the body permanently weakened, yet although there are lingering disabilities, the disease itself may no longer remain even chronically in the body.

After a similar pattern, the sin-disease in racial humanity has marred and maimed our human constitution, physically, mentally, morally, spiritually. . . . As the children of Adam's fallen family, we cannot avoid our inheritance of those racial deteriorations which we commonly call "our natural infirmities". But (let us underscore it) those "natural infirmities" are not in themselves sin; they are the transmitted results of it. Even inherited sinward *propensities* are not themselves sin in any sense which makes us *guilty*—for "guilt" is a legal concept and has to do solely with transgression; neither do they preclude real holiness, seeing that holiness is not "faultlessness" but "blamelessness".

I know a certain druggist and his wife whose young son was the most cantankerous little rascal ever born in the English county of Yorkshire. They were scared lest he should ever sneak behind the counter in the drug store and get his meddlesome little fingers on any bottles containing poison. They used to warn him severely, but to a rascally young mind like his, the prohibition only inflamed the temptation. One day when his parents were temporarily absent, he prowled into the forbidden territory, and stalked off with two bottles from the lowest shelf, which he could just reach. Then, with these two captures, he had a wonderful time in the living-room just behind the store, making a pattern on his mother's best white linen tablecloth. The contents of one bottle made a succession of big, bluey-black splodges up and down the cloth. The contents of the other bottle burnt holes through it! When his mother returned, I am not sure where the greater suffering occurred—in her mind, or on his anatomy. Perhaps the most diplomatic way to report what happened is to say that she forcibly applied the "hand of wisdom" to the "seat of learning"! Then she quickly took the cloth, and in the good old-fashioned way "rub-adub-dubbed" it with soap and bleaches in the washtub. Then she rinsed it, and put it through the wringer, and hung it out on a line in the backyard. There it hung, in the evening breeze and sunshine, perfectly clean again, every one of those big, ugly, bluey-black stains washed away. But, oh!—nearly a dozen gaping holes! You can wash stains out; but no soap or detergent on earth can wash *holes* out! Even so is it in this matter of experiential sanctification. Sin, so to speak, has made "holes" in our nature; call them "natural infirmities" or what you will; but, thank God, these do not render cleansing and purity impossible. There can be real holiness in spite of them, and co-existent with them. The cloth can be cleansed despite holes! The sanctification to which God calls us is not faultlessness but *blamelessness*.

The big question still remaining is: How can this holiness, this inward cleansing of motive, this blamelessness, become real and *experiential* within us? Again Ephesians 1: 4, comes to our aid. God chose us, it says, before the foundation of the world, "that we should be holy, even without blame, before Him *in love*". That little phrase, "in love", is like the release-clasp on a jewel-case, which springs the lid open and discloses the jewel within. The whole secret of holiness is here suddenly opened up and simplified. The way into it is *love*, that is, the heart and mind flooded and suffused by the love of Christ. When heart and mind are thus filled with love, all the motives become cleansed and pure; for as the Word says, "Love worketh no ill to his neighbour; therefore love is the fulfilling of the law" (Rom. 13: 10). "All the law is fulfilled in one word, even in this: Thou shalt love . . ." (Gal. 5: 14). Yes, as heart and mind become filled with love, all the *motives* become pure; and when all the motives are pure, that is *blamelessness*; and such moral blamelessness is true *holiness*.

We cannot compel our *own* love suddenly to enlarge itself into unprecedented volume, for love is one of those qualities or out-reaches of heart which come either spontaneously or not at all. Nor can we wave some magic wand to bring into existence a love which was not within us heretofore. What we *can* do is to yield ourselves in such reverent abandon to God's dear Son that *His* great love may unobstructedly express itself in and through us. When we do this, not merely in spasmodic crises, but in prayerful continuity, the continuing infusion of our Lord's love both purifies and increases our *own* love, calling into activity capacities of compassion which beforehand we never suspected were in our nature. Our Lord's love thus finds ever-widening channels through our consecrated personalities, and in its pure depths our own love becomes ever deeper and richer.

Evangelical holiness is never merely negative—an abstention from sin. Rather, it is positive—a being actuated by beneficent *love*. All too many Christian believers are spending themselves in an unequal struggle to oust inborn evil biases from their nature. Yet even if they could completely succeed (which they never do) they would by that means create only a vacuum. True holiness is no such vacuum; it is the heart captivated, dominated, per-meated, renovated, motivated by the glorious love of Christ. This is the richest form of self-realisation. Egocentricity gives place to

Christocentricity; the whole life becomes sublimated in *His* life. Personality becomes inwardly and then outwardly transfigured as we learn more and more the Pauline secret, "I live, yet not I, but Christ liveth in me; and the life which I now live in the flesh, I live by faith of the Son of God, who loved me, and gave Himself for me" (Gal. 2: 20). His love *toward* us now becomes His love *within* us; and its expulsive power "casts out" fear (1 John 4: 18) along with the whole unruly brood—pride, anger, jealousy, lust, selfishness.

James 2: 8 says, "If ye fulfil *the royal law* according to the Scriptures: Thou shalt *love* thy neighbour as thyself, ye shall do well." Mark that expression, "the royal law". In our present condition, we are not under the precise law which conditioned unfallen Adam in his Edenic perfection. Nor can we by the utmost merely natural exertion, fulfil even the law of Moses in its spiritual interpretation. God has therefore adapted a law which is congenial to our defective constitution. In the phraseology of James, it is "the royal law" of *love*. There is nothing of legal bondage or stern whip about it. It is a law which we keep, not because we legally *must,* but because we gratefully *may*; not because we fear, but because we *love*. That is why, four verses later, James calls it "the law of *liberty*". In Galatians 6: 2, Paul calls it "the law of *Christ*"—"Bear ye one another's burdens, and so fulfil the law of Christ." It is the spontaneous keeping of *that* law which gives "blamelessness" and holiness; and the secret of keeping it is in Romans 5: 5, "The love of God is *shed abroad* in our hearts by the Holy Spirit which is given unto us".

An obvious corollary of this is, that true holiness simply cannot be drab, sour, torrid, frigid, or gloomy. What is more kindly, forbearing, sympathetic, joyful, or radiant than real *love?* "Love suffereth long, and is kind. Love vaunteth not itself, is never puffed up. . . . Beareth all things, believeth all things, hopeth all things, endureth all things. Love never faileth" (1 Cor. 13). This being filled, cleansed, constrained by the love of Christ banishes sombreness and melancholy. Our sun never goes down; the Lord is our "everlasting light" and the "days of our mourning" are "ended" (Isa. 60: 19, 20).

So, then, to sum up: God has pre-elected us in Christ with a view to our present and future sanctification or *holiness.* The holiness to which God calls us, and which He makes possible for us, in the present, is not faultlessness, *but blamelessness,* which consists in the thorough purifying of all our motives—Godward, manward, selfward. This inward purifying and blamelessness come through our being renewed *in* and motivated *by* love—the love of Christ infilling and suffusing us, quickening and enriching our own moral and spiritual capacities, and conforming us to His own image. Oh, this blessed privilege of heaven-provided sanctification! Oh, to be filled to overflow with the pure, gentle, mighty love of Jesus "shed abroad in our hearts by the Holy Spirit"!

Christian believer, adore and wonder at this highest of all spiritual mysteries: you *may really be filled with the love of God.* "The love of God is shed abroad in our hearts by the Holy Spirit" (Rom. 5: 5). Once the spiritual splendour of it breaks on our minds we never recover from the everlasting surprise of it. The only reason why most of us read a verse like Romans 5: 5 without amazement is that we skim it with hurried familiarity, hardly crediting that it really means what it says.

When it says that the "love of God" is shed within us, it means, not merely a sensing of God's love *toward* us, but the very love which God has (and is) transfused *within* us!

Moffatt's magnetic translation of 1 John 4: 18 draws me again and again—"*Love in its fulness drives all dread away.*" Dear Christian, ponder it well: that "love in its fulness", pervading, purifying, suffusing and renewing the mind, is holiness in its highest, deepest, sublimest aspect. It is *"ENTIRE SANCTIFICATION"*.

That "love in its fulness" not only ejects all tormenting fear, it chastens, refines, enriches and beautifies the whole character. It brings cloudless fellowship with the heavenly Father, and lifts the Christian life into a sunlit Emmaus walk with the risen Lord. It not only exposes sin in its real ugliness to the clarified inner perception of the believer; it becomes an invincible expulsive power against every unholy imagination. It not only quickens the soul in every holy desire, it *satisfies* all that holy hunger. Christ becomes to us in living experience "the Fulness of God" (Eph. 3: 19). It transforms our whole outlook on holiness from a legalistic *"must I?"* to an affectionate *"may I?"* It turns selfishness into generosity, and egocentricity into Christlike otherism. It does away with the last rag of mere professionalism, and restores us to humble, downright reality. The yoke of Jesus no longer chafes. The last remnant of subtle servility is banished. The will of God becomes our glad, spontaneous choice. Suddenly we find large freedom in "the law of liberty", the "royal law" (Jas. 1: 25, 2: 8); not escape *from* the will of God, but spacious, satisfying freedom *in* it. When we are living in the experience of this "love in its fulness" we break into singing,

> "Oh, the peace my Saviour gives!
> Peace I never knew before!"

> "I have found the joy no tongue can tell,
> How its waves of glory roll!"

> "I've reached the land of corn and wine,
> Its blessings all are freely mine!"

But are you still asking: How do I *enter* this covetable experience? Let me offer sympathetic counsel. It is no use, of itself, bracing your *will* to secure it, or trying intensely to make yourself *feel* it, or laying down rules supposed to *bring* it. No, it never comes by *any* reflexive action of the soul upon itself, any more than we could propel a boat by puffing at the sails with our own breath. Someone has said, "Love is the only word convertible with God". Accordingly, the way into this blessing of "love in its fulness" is that we *receive GOD*. We must open to Him all the avenues of our being; every room of the house; every key to every door and cupboard; for even one reservation means that we do not completely trust Him. Once the whole being is thrown open for the Divine occupancy, the blessing becomes ours by an appropriating absorption.

Look at Romans 5: 5 again: "The love of God is *shed abroad* in our hearts by the Holy Spirit." Obviously, so copious an in-shedding of divine love must be a *conscious* experience. It may not bring sudden transports of sensory rapture or emotional ecstasy, but it *must* register itself in one's clear *awareness*. Its accompaniments differ in varying dispositions and circumstances, but when it really happens it is certainly *felt*. As to the manner of its attesting itself, my advice is always: Leave that to the Holy Spirit.

Get alone with God—often enough, long enough. He may not keep you waiting; but He wisely may. All depends on the utterness of your self-yielding; and it often takes longer for many of us to get *there* than it does for God to *meet* us there. My belief is, that once you are really *there,* you will find yourself receiving, with wonderful naturalness, what God is freely offering.

The saintly John Fletcher tells how *he* sought the blessing. Eventually it came. "The Lord for whom I had waited came suddenly to the temple of my heart, and I had immediate evidence that this was the blessing which I had for some time been seeking." In his case there was a vivid accompaniment, for he continues, "I then received the full witness of the Spirit. . . . My heart was softened and warmed and filled; my prayer was turned into praises, and I could do nothing but shout 'Glory be to God!' "

Dear Christian, it may or may not happen like that to *you*. Leave that with God. Get alone with Jesus until the whole universe is shut out, and in the silent aloneness you are heart to heart. Yield your *all*. Mean it, and *do* it, whether emotionally you are in the tropic or arctic or temperate zone (the last is the best for such deep-going and far-reaching transaction). Tell Him you want Romans 5: 5, not for selfish enjoyment of an "experience", but in order to be truly *holy* according to Ephesians 1: 4; and in order to reflect *His* life through your personality; and in order to be so freed from selfism that your liberated heart goes out in healing sympathies to the needy ones all around you. Keep your eyes on the *promise* of the blessing. "Though it tarry, wait for it; because it will surely come" (Hab. 2: 3). And let your prayer be,

> Break through my nature, mighty heavenly love ;
> Clear every avenue of thought and brain ;
> Flood my affections, purify my will ;
> Make *all I am* Thy sanctified domain.
>
> Thus, wholly mastered and by Thee possessed,
> Forth from my life, spontaneous and free,
> Shall flow a stream of tenderness and grace ;
> Loving, because *Thy* love now lives in *me*.

SANCTIFICATION:
SOME HIGH INCENTIVES

Lord, set me fully free from sin,
   For now I plainly see,
Howe'er it wrongs my fellowmen,
   Far more it pierces Thee.

My sin! ah, now I understand,
   It flouts Thy heaven above,
Not merely breaking Thy command,
   But wounding Thy great love.

I little knew this till I saw
   The holy love Thou art;
Sin does not only break Thy law,
   It broke Thy very heart!

It cost Thy Calv'ry anguish sore,
   Its hateful curse to bear!
Oh, most of all do I deplore
   To see it nail Thee there!

O God, my broken accents hear;
   My mind and heart refine,
Till all within me mirrors clear
   My Saviour-King divine!

                          J.S.B.

SANCTIFICATION:
SOME HIGH INCENTIVES

"What manner of persons ought ye to be, in all holy conversation and godliness?" (2 Pet. 3: 11).

THIS is the sixth link in our chain of reflections on the theme of sanctification. Having pondered the salient first meanings, we ought now to be challenged by some of the impressive New Testament *persuasives* to sanctification.

Purpose of the Church's Bridegroom

Of these, perhaps the first we should mention is, that our sanctification is *the dearest intention of the heavenly Bridegroom*. Read Ephesians 5: 25–27 again, slowly and thoughtfully.

"Christ also loved the Church, and gave Himself for it, that He might *sanctify* and cleanse it with the washing of water by the Word; that He might present it to Himself a glorious Church, not having spot or wrinkle or any such thing; but that it should be *holy and without blemish*."

Admit·edly this exalted picture of the Church has its ultimate reference to the age-end rapture and consummation of the Church corporate; yet does that in any way diminish its implication for the present? Nay; for if the heavenly Bridegroom purposes our utter holiness *then*, does He not intend our utmost holiness *now*? And if He purposes holiness for the Church collectively, does not that imply a like intention for believers individually?

The clause, "That He might sanctify and cleanse it . . ." should read, as in later translations, "That He might sanctify it, *having* cleansed it. . . ." Those other words, "the washing of water by the Word", are a pictorial reference to *regeneration*. Clearly, then, our Lord's purpose is, that having *regenerated* us here and now, He might also *sanctify* us here and now.

That this Ephesian delineation of the Church does indeed intend our present, individual sanctification is made clearer if we separate Paul's successive clauses.

1. "Christ loved the Church ;"
   —that is a mystery of eternity.
2. "And gave Himself for it ;"
   —that is a verity of history.
3. "To sanctify it, having cleansed it ;"
   —that is a purpose in the present.
4. "That He might present it to Himself . . ."
   —that is a finale of the future.

The truth is, that although this passage views the Church in its corporate and historical totality, it none the less pre-envisages believers individually, as the context shows. The Church corporate and historical is made up of Christian individuals. There can be no sanctified Church without sanctified individual believers. The true Church consists of all those human beings who, by simple yet vital faith, are savingly united to Christ, whatever may be their temporary varieties of denomination. Never yet has the whole Church been on earth. Only a fraction of it is on earth today. Millions of its members have already passed through and beyond earthly scenes into the paradise above. Millions of its elect members are yet unborn, or are yet unconverted. But there is always *some* part of the Ecclesia on earth. This, then, is our Lord's purpose and desire: As the historical Church, in its successive generations, passes through this transitional earth-phase to its heavenly translation, every individual member of it shall be not only regenerated by the "washing of the Word", but *sanctified,* and filled with the "Spirit of Holiness".

Perhaps not even the most spiritually minded among us have yet suspected how *tender* is the divine-human love of the Lord Jesus for those who comprise His mystic bride. The Gospel records tell us how, again and again, He was "moved with compassion" toward the multitude, but they also reveal beyond any mistaking that he had a specially *tender* love for those who were the inner circle of "His own". The thirteenth chapter of John's Gospel begins, "Jesus knowing that His hour had come that He should depart out of this world unto the Father, having loved His own which were in the world, He loved them unto the end". The Greek word here translated as "unto the end" really means "to the *uttermost*". Although our translators have felt that the context required them to translate it as "unto the end", the stronger reference of the word is not to time but to degree. To my own mind it is better even contextually to read it, "He loved them unto the *uttermost*", for it is followed immediately by our Lord's loving lowliness in washing the disciples' feet, and then by those wonderful Bethany chapters in which, with opened heart, He tells them of His love as never before (13: 34, 14: 21, 15: 9, 10, 12, 13).

That same tender love is still in His heart toward "His own which are in the world". As Hebrews 7: 25 says, "He ever liveth to make intercession" for us, which implies, of course, that we are continually in His thought, on His heart, and in His love. What is it, then, that His tender-hearted love for us most desires? It is this, that having become regenerated through "the washing of water by the Word", we should become *sanctified* through entire yieldedness to Him, and by the infilling of the Holy Spirit.

Is there anything more urgently needed among the churches today than a recall to this individual sanctification? Was there ever more regimentation with less sanctification? The late Dr. A. J. Gordon of Boston once wrote: "A noble head, lofty-browed and intellectual, upon a deformed and stunted body is a pitiable sight. Even so, an unsanctified church dishonours the Lord by its incongruity. To the angels and principalities who gaze evermore upon the face of Jesus, what must be the sight of an unholy and misshapen church on earth, standing in that place of honour called 'His body'?"

Object of Divine Election.

A second great incentive to sanctification is *our election thereto by God the Father*. Turn back again to Ephesians 1: 4, "According as He [God] hath chosen us in Him [Christ] before the foundation of the world, that we should be holy, even without blame before Him in love". In the outer world of nature there are some phenomena which cause perpetual astonishment to the beholder. I think it was the philosopher-traveller, Humboldt, who said he could never look out across the rolling Prairies without indescribable emotion. Never can I forget the overpowering effect on my own mind when Mont Blanc and the Chamonix Valley first swung into view as we rounded the bend of an Alpine road. Others have been spellbound by the florid splendours of a

Mediterranean sunset, or overawed by the starry magnitudes of a translucent night sky. Yet what are all the marvels of the physical realm, compared with this divine wonder of our pre-election into the mystic bride of Christ before time itself began?

Those words, "Before the foundation of the world" seem to refer to the beginning of the solid earth itself, not only to the "cosmos", or system of life upon it. What is the age of this planet? According to modern science it is not so young as used to be thought. Some years ago, when I was in the pastoral ministry, I began to notice a certain well-known scientist attending our Sunday services. He was one of the most brilliant and capaciously informed intellectuals I ever knew. Not only did his academic distinctions make him a kind of alpha-star, dazzling to the lesser stars and satellites who covetously twinkled in and around his constellation, but he was verily a walking encyclopædia of scientific knowledge. He was a member of the British Association of Scientists, a member and lecturer at the Victoria Institute, and was considered one of the nation's leading geologists and zoologists, not to mention other distinguishments. What that supernormal brain of his did not know about geology, biology, zoology, anthropology, ethnology and other kindred "ologies", who should tell him? As for myself, whenever he was present, I made sure that in my preaching I carefully avoided all doubtful matters geological, biological, zoological, anthropological, ethnological, and other-ological. In short, I kept to what is sometimes called "the simple Gospel"; and I have a pleasant suspicion that this was why he kept coming to worship with us. However, one Sunday morning, I must inadvertently have blundered a tip-toe into one of his august domains! Immediately after the service he strode into my vestry, and in his husky but imperious way asked, "Sir, do you know what is the consensus of modern scientific opinion concerning the antiquity of our earth?" I had to confess that at the moment it eluded me, whereupon he continued, "The present consensus of scientific opinion is that this earth of ours is approximately three hundred million years old". All I could think of replying was, "What a marvel! It means, according to Ephesians 1: 4, that God chose you and me in Christ *more than three hundred million years ago!*"

I suppose that even "three hundred million" would now be considered much behind the times. Based on the "Second Law of Thermodynamics" (i.e. entropy, the gradual loss of heat or energy in the material universe) scientists now determine an approximate date of 4.5 *billion* years ago for the formation of our planet and its neighbours. This established fact of gradual decay in the elements (for instance, the gradual decay of the radio-active elements, uranium and thorium, into helium and lead) not only indicates the *date* of beginning, but the *fact* of a beginning, i.e. an original *creation* as according to Genesis 1: 1. Put those two things together: first, our earth and its surrounding systems began 4.5 billion (or four thousand five hundred million) years ago; second, the statement of our text that God fore-chose us in Christ *before* that, even "before the foundation of the world"! We can but exclaim again: either it is the veriest fairy tale, or it is the most stupendous mystery of divine compassion and sovereignty ever divulged on this little earth to our race of mankind.

Yes, ponder it, Christian believer: between four and five billion years ago you and I were in the thought and choice of God. Perhaps putting it like that makes it more startling to our minds. It is a sheer mystery of divine love, and one of the supreme surprises of Biblical revelation. That He, the uncreated, eternal Creator of all things, the omniscient, omnipresent, infinite *GOD* of the universe, should from pre-cosmic depths set His electing love, upon you and me—infinitesimal creatures that we seem to be, and sin-deformed, ill-deserving transgressors, is surely the super-marvel of all mysteries! Does it not subdue us into adoring gratitude and reverent yearning to be all that God *meant* us to be? What was it, then, that was uppermost in the divine purpose concerning you and me, more than four billion years ago? It was this: "That we should be *holy, even without blame before Him in love.*" Is not *that* an overpowering incentive to sanctification?

Our Saviour's Special Prayer

Turn now to John 17, to the intercessory prayer which Jesus prayed for His disciples just before He crossed the Kedron into Gethsemane. In verse 17 He prays, "Sanctify them through Thy truth; Thy word is truth." So our sanctification is the special request of the Son to the Father. Is not that another persuasive to consecration and holiness?

What comfort there is for us in that prayer of our Saviour!
It shows how His people were on His heart now that He was
about to leave the world and return to the Father. No surprise
could have been occasioned if His mind had been too filled with
His own impending agony and crucifixion to be praying for
others. It should stir up our deep and grateful wonder all the
more, to see how, even in that dark hour, He must pour out His
heart for His own people.

The prayer, throughout, breathes the most tender solicitude
toward all His disciples; and it reaches right down through the
years, to you and me; for in verse 20 He says, "Neither do I
pray for these alone, but for them also which shall believe on
Me through their word". Moreover, this prayer, coming right at
the end of our Lord's ministry on earth, indicates the kind of
prayers He now prays for us as our ascended High Priest in the
heavenly sanctuary. What, then, does He pray for us? He prays
outstandingly for four things:

1. Our *preservation*:
    "I pray not that Thou shouldst take them out
    of the world, but that Thou shouldst keep
    them from the evil" (15).

2. Our *sanctification*:
    "Sanctify them through Thy truth: Thy
    word is truth" (17).

3. Our *unification*:
    "That they all may be one, as Thou, Father,
    art in Me, and I in Thee" (21).

4. Our *glorification*:
    "That they also be with Me where I am, that
    they may behold My glory" (24).

The preservation which our Lord asks is no mere preservation
from physical trouble, but from moral evil. The sanctification
which He wants for us is no mere monastic reclusion, but a
separatedness to the divine will and service (see verse 18). The
unification which He prays for is no mere external uniformity
of organization, but an inward and spiritual oneness. If we think
of the many other things which our Lord *might* have asked for
us, but did not, we soon see which things *He* considers most
important. Mere physical immunities or advantages He never
once mentions. It is our *spiritual* wellbeing which dominates His
all-wise, all-loving concern. The centre-point is His beseeching

the Father to *sanctify* us; for without such sanctification there can be no preservation of believers from worldly "evil"; nor can there be any real unification making all believers "one"; nor can there be final glorification, apart from "the sanctification without which no man shall see the Lord" (Heb. 12: 14).

"They are not of this world," He says. "Keep them from the evil." "Sanctify them through Thy truth: Thy word is truth." This was our Saviour's parting prayer for His own, as He came to the hour of His own departure. This was the concern uppermost in His mind *then*, and which is therefore uppermost in His mind *now*. Shall His prayer be answered in you and me? Or shall we lazily risk postponing sanctification until (as many presumptuously mis-suppose) our eventual "translation" somehow confers it upon us? What a grief to His heart must such gratuitous neglect be!

Sanctification Really Possible.

We mention just one other of these New Testament persuasives to sanctification. In 1 Corinthians 1: 30 we read, "But of Him [God] are ye in Christ Jesus, who is made unto us wisdom from God, even righteousness and sanctification and redemption." Over against the spiritually blind "wisdom of this world", which did not even recognise the Lord of Glory when He trod the earth, Christ is our *true* "Wisdom". He is so in a threefold, soul-saving way. He is made unto us (1) *"righteousness"*—a new standing of imputed righteousness before God; (2) *"sanctification"*—a new condition of imparted holiness in mind and heart; (3) *"redemption"*—which here has a forward look to our bodily transfiguration at the reappearing of Christ.

The vital fact here stated is, that Christ is *"made"* unto us "sanctification". That is what makes sanctification really possible for us, despite all the problems of our inherited perversity and deviousness. It underscores our repeated insistence that holiness, in its experiential reality, is not a state of self-control or sin-control which we somehow *achieve* by strenuous struggle of the self with itself, but a supernatural *renewal* of mind and heart, of motive and inclination, inwrought by the Holy Spirit. Yes, that is what makes true sanctification possible and effectual. The mind-elevating miracle is indeed appropriable to the fully yielded and receptive heart. Even as every other spiritual enrichment provided for us is "in *Him*", so is it with sanctification; and the reason we keep on emphasizing this is because so many of us keep on doubting it, thereby frustrating our own prayers for the blessing.

Just as, at our conversion, we received forgiveness and justification by faith, so must we now appropriate *holiness* by faith. There are texts which plainly tell us so. Observe the word, "faith", in the following verses which specifically concern receiving the Holy Spirit and holiness. In Galatians 3: 2 Paul asks, "Received ye the Spirit by the works of the law, or through *faith?*" In verse 14 he himself answers that question, in the words, "We receive the promise of the Spirit through *faith*". In Acts 15: 8, 9, we read, "And God, which knoweth the hearts, bare them witness, giving them the Holy Spirit . . . purifying their hearts through *faith*". And again, in Acts 26: 18, where Paul recounts our Lord's words to him on the Damascus road, we have the clause, "Them that are sanctified by *faith*", i.e. faith in our Lord Jesus. Our salvation is not a part-salvation in which we are regenerated through faith and then left to struggle after holiness in our own strength—or weakness. No! as 1 Corinthians 1: 30, says, Christ is *"made* unto us . . . sanctification". We may crystallise it in fourfold statement. Sanctification is—

1. In Christ (1 Cor. 1: 30; Eph. 1: 4).
2. Via the Word (John 17: 17; Eph. 5: 26).
3. Through faith (Gal. 3: 14; Acts 26: 18).
4. By the Holy Spirit (Rom. 15: 16).

It is so easy to analyse and state these precious truths; but oh, how reverently should we contemplate them, and relate ourselves to them! They represent to us the holy, heavenly calling to which God has called us, and show us how graciously God has provided to make it possible for us to walk the "way of holiness". We do well to heed the caution of Hebrews 4: 1, "Let us therefore fear, lest a promise being left us . . . any of us should seem to come short of it". Let it be our eager longing and persevering prayer that we may "possess our possessions", and begin to explore these "heavenly places in Christ".

The Four-leaved Gateway

Does someone say, "I long to enter the blessing, and to live the sanctified life, but somehow I still am not clear *how*"? Well, perhaps it may help if we add this final word. Whatever our theories of sanctification may be, when it comes to a practical *experience* of it, we all find that it follows a fourfold pattern:

1. When I really yield myself to Christ, He really sets me apart for His possession and use. That is the crisis by which I *become* sanctified in the sense of complete set-apartness.
2. As I maintain this yieldedness, so that the initial crisis becomes a continuing process, I *remain* sanctified in this same sense of complete set-apartness.
3. Upon my being thus yielded entirely and continually to Christ, He begins to fill me by the Holy Spirit, and continues to do so, whether I am always emotionally conscious of this or not.
4. As the Holy Spirit thus fills me, He purifies my motives and desires, refines my nature, corrects evil proclivities, makes Christ luminous to my mind, expands my spiritual capacities, and so atmospheres me that I become Christ-communicative to others. This is *inwrought* sanctification.

The first two of these four mainly concern the *human* side of sanctification. The other two are the *divine* side. The four thus go together reciprocally. It is no use "claiming" 3 and 4, unless we are fulfilling 1 and 2; but if we are fulfilling 1 and 2, we may confidently appropriate and expect 3 and 4.

Cautionary Counsels

Sometimes in meetings for the deepening of the spiritual life, Christians are asked to stand, as an outward sign of their now having surrendered themselves entirely to Christ. Many believers *do* so yield themselves in such meetings, only to find later, alas, that somehow their sacred transaction has seemingly proved evanescent, causing them to wonder whether they really *did* yield themselves to Christ after all. The reason for most such disappointments is that there has been one vital element lacking. Even the grateful and adoring love which prompts my entire self-surrender to Christ must be crowned by an act of *faith*. That is, I must believe that what I really *give*, He really *takes*. I may need to say it a thousand times to myself: "I really gave myself to Him; I therefore believe that He has really taken me, and set me apart." This, so to speak, *clinches* the transaction in our minds. We count it settled as between ourselves and Him, and believe that He now controls.

Another thing ever to remember is that this self-yielding to Christ must continue day by day, and hour by hour, and even minute by minute. Since you and I are finite, it is obvious that in the sacred crisis of our first full-yielding to Christ, we cannot think of everything at once, or know for certain even one day ahead. Every new day something will crop up of which we are obliged to say, "I was not thinking of that when I dedicated all to Christ". Yet this does not mean that those unforeseeable items were not included. On the contrary, we are to say in each such instance, "I may not have been thinking particularly about this at the time, and I could not foresee this circumstance, but it was anticipated in the one, all-inclusive hand-over, and I must now therefore at once put it on the altar with all the rest."

The Altar Sanctifieth

When we are really living in that consecrated way, we need have no hesitation in considering ourselves sanctified, in the sense that our Saviour has actually set us apart specially for Himself. Remember our Lord's words in Matthew 23: 19, "The altar sanctifieth the gift". When an Israelite laid an offering on the temple altar, his gift immediately became sanctified thereby. So is it the moment you and I become fully given up to Christ as "living sacrifices": *immediately* "the altar sanctifieth the gift". Dear Christian, believe it; act upon it; and if afterward you still experience tendencies, motives, or actual failings which seem to belie it, *still* dare to believe it; for it is as we maintain this human side of sanctification that it becomes complemented, either suddenly or more gradually, by the promised *divine* activity of the infilling Holy Spirit.

Alas, nagging at my heart as I say these things, is the saddening awareness that many whom I now address have known this doctrine and heard such advice so long and so often that their nodding approval now means no more than agreement *theoretically*. There are many evangelical ministers and others who hold to a "position" on sanctification yet do not honestly believe any longer in sanctification as an actual work of the Holy Spirit consciously *experienced* in the soul. Oh, that all such might be aroused to see how they are grieving the Saviour! —impoverishing themselves! —hindering the Spirit! —blocking their own spiritual usefulness!

And there is yet one further cautionary word which we must add. When the Holy Spirit begins to infill and renew the inner being of the consecrated believer, there are times when His sanctifying activity will excite the emotions into a godly exuberance. There will be an emotional *attestation* of our sanctification. But we must not be deluded into thinking that sanctification *consists* in such emotional exhilarations. All too many Christian believers miss much of the blessing because they seek a vivid "experience" rather than a vital *deliverance*. They forget that the Holy Spirit comes to do His most important work, not in the emotions, but in the *character*. Our emotions are the most volatile part of us. If we are to know a settled poise of mind, the emotions must always be in subordination to intellect and will. Our "experience" will always be mercurial if we pay too much attention to our emotions. It is inward deliverance from sin, and likeness to Jesus in our character, which *vitally* matter. Too many emotional raptures and sensory ecstasies would be a doubtful luxury for these delicate nervous systems of ours.

When our Lord told the disciples that after His own departure the Paraclete would come to them, He said, "He shall glorify Me"; and above all else the Holy Spirit seeks to do that in and through the sanctified believer. Moses "wist not" that His face shone; but it *shone* none the less. Even so, the main thing in our sanctification is not that we shall be continually indulged in excitement of mere "feelings", but that Christ shall become "glorified" through a Spirit-wrought likeness to Him. Emotional accompaniments there certainly will be, if we are prayerfully maintaining a sanctified life; but more often than not, I think, the attestations will be in the nature of a deep, wondrous peace, or assurance, or Christ-consciousness rather than in irrepressible ejaculations of exhilaration. Much depends, however, on our natural constitution and its characteristic reactions.

Meanwhile, the great thing to realise, as we have said, is that the Spirit's deepest work is in the *character*, not in the emotions. Sanctification is meant to effect moral and spiritual transformation—and that is what real sanctification always does. My beloved friend, the late Dr. Rowland V. Bingham, once told us the following incident which had first been narrated to himself by the veteran missionary, Canon Burns of Nairobi. A poor old woman had been taken by her people and thrown into the long grass outside the village because she was now too sick to help herself any more. That is the easy way of the folk out there when dealing with the aged and helpless. Mrs. Burns, who was a trained nurse, happened to hear of the poor old woman's plight, and managed to find the spot where she had been left to die. There the old body was, a mass of sores, dirty, helpless, and surrounded by swarms of insects. Mrs. Burns tried to persuade the people to bring the sick woman back to one of their little market sheds, but there was no response to this until she used the money appeal. There, in a market shed, with a kindly nurse's touch, Mrs. Burns washed the sores and gently applied healing ointment. She also supplied nourishment, and effected what protection she could from the flies. Then, leaving food, she promised to return in the morning. Day after day the loving treatment was repeated; and each day Mrs. Burns told a little more about the love of God and about Jesus the Saviour of sinners. Little by little the poor sick body responded to the food and the medicine and the tender nursing. One morning when Mrs. Burns returned, the old woman was sitting up, wonderfully better, a radiant smile on her face, and she greeted her benefactor with the surprising words, "Your Jesus came to me last night. Yes, He came right to me, and I knew him; but the strange thing was—*He had your face!*"

Oh, may we never forget that whatever periodic emotional raptures accompany a life of Spirit-wrought sanctification, its most authentic evidence is always the transfiguration of our *character*. That is the Holy Spirit's greatest work within us. That is what God more than all else desires. That is what most of all honours and recommends our dear Lord. That is what blesses the needy human hearts all around us as nothing else can. That, indeed, is our high calling. Well may our oft-repeated prayer be:

Live in my living; think through all my thought,
Will through my will till only Thine is wrought;
Move through each impulse, temper each desire,
Cleanse all my motives in Thy heavenly fire.

Speak through my speaking; love in all my love;
Shed through each feeling fragrance from above;
Come, blest Shekinah, flame throughout my mind,
Till, cleansed from dross, I am as gold refined.

Bid high aspirings in my heart awake,
And my whole life Thy worthier dwelling make;
Come, with Thy heavenly, sin-consuming flame,
And for Thy temple my whole being claim.

Part Two
Errors About Sanctification

NOTE

Some of the errors about sanctification which
we examine in this second part of our treatise
are of long standing. For that reason some of
their most powerful proponents belong to days
now past. Yet it must not be therefore supposed
that the errors themselves are now dead. On the
contrary, in various respects they are very much
alive. Their able originators and expounders,
although no longer on earth, are still quoted as
authorities; and their influence on the thinking
of all too many concerning sanctification still
survives with strangely persistent power to be-
guile.

Perhaps, too, at this point, a word of explanation may be appropriate. Much as we dislike the
controversial it cannot be avoided in chapters
on "Errors"; so let two things be made clear:

(1) These errors are dealt with at the urging
of Christian believers who have been perplexed
by the teachings here examined.

(2) Some of those whom we presume to counter,
like the famous C. G. Finney and those two
Princeton giants Charles and Alexander Hodge,
are among our most admired heroes of the
recent past. Therefore any criticism here ventured is purely exegetical, *never* personal. Our
diverging from them in one particular aspect
in nowise lessens our thankfulness to God for the
grandeur of their ministry as a whole. If we
speak frankly it is always with frankness steeped
in esteem.

J.S.B.

"I recollect great complaint being made against a sermon of mine, 'Compel them to come in', which I spake with much tenderness for souls. That sermon was said to be Arminian and unsound. Brethren, it is a small matter to me to be judged of men's judgment, for my Master has set his seal on that message. I never preached a sermon by which so many souls were won to God, as our Church meetings can testify; and all over the world, where the sermon has been scattered, sinners have been saved through its instrumentality; and, therefore, if it be vile to exhort sinners, I purpose to be viler still. I am as firm a believer in the doctrines of grace as any living man, and a true Calvinist after the order of John Calvin himself; but if it be thought an evil thing to bid the sinner lay hold on eternal life, I will be yet more evil in this respect, and herein imitate my Lord and his apostles, who, though they taught that salvation is of grace, and grace alone, feared not to speak to men as rational beings and responsible agents, and bid them 'strive to enter in at the strait gate', and 'labour not for the meat which perisheth, but for that meat which endureth unto everlasting life'. Beloved friends, cling to the great truth of electing love and divine sovereignty, but let not these bind you in fetters when, in the power of the Holy Ghost, you become fishers of men."

C. H. Spurgeon.

To my own mind this was very *healthy* Calvinism.

J.S.B.

SANCTIFICATION AND CALVINISM

ONE of the marvels of history is the persistent dominance of the Christian faith despite all the oppositions of determined foes. I sometimes think that an equal wonder is its triumph over the well-meaning misrepresentations of its *friends*. It was an eye-opener to me, when I first delved into Church history, to find that many of the worst heretics were the sincerest of believers, and that the progenitors of the most subtle extremisms have nearly always been persons of keen spiritual-mindedness.

Scarcely is there any distinctive doctrine of Christianity, but it has been strained, wrenched, distorted, travestied, not by critics *outside* the Christian pale, but by champions *inside*. Ever since Peter impulsively lopped off Malchus's ear in Gethsemane, mistakenly thinking he did Christ service, our Lord has been correcting the well-meant errors of disciples whose zeal has out-run sound exegesis of His Word. Nor has such zeal always been erratic or unscholarly. It has been truly said: "Scarcely an error can be named that some learned doctor has not advocated and supported by his texts."

Some of these errors are like bogs with a deceptive upper appearance of solid footing. Others are like precipices with edges concealed by pleasant flowers and greenery. Others are like John Bunyan's "By-path Meadow"—innocent looking little short-cuts to a seemingly superior spirituality. Others are like road-signs marked, "This way to Blessing-town", but pointing the wrong way. Especially in this matter of sanctification, or holiness, we need to be on our guard against the fond illusions of the sincere and the scholarly, as well as the merely plausible. Paul has a remarkable little phrase in 1 Timothy 2: 15, "Sanctification with *sobriety*"! It is wise that we should be intelligently informed against exaggerated or aberrant *theories* of sanctification. On some of these we are now going to hang our warning sign: "BEWARE"; and to begin with we shall notice certain *defective concepts of sin*; for as has been truly said, if we are rightly to apply a remedy we must properly know the malady.

CALVINISTIC CONFUSIONS

I myself am Calvinistic in general theological persuasion which, however, does not mean that I agree with John Calvin in every detail of his dicta; much less does it mean that I go along with some of the ideas propagated by others under the aegis of Calvinism.

Let me give sincere caution against that Calvinistic view of sin which makes experiential sanctification practically an impossibility. I refer, for instance, to those Princeton giants of yesterday, Drs. Charles Hodge (*Systematic Theology*, in three volumes) and Alexander A. Hodge, his son (*Outlines of Theology*), both of them massive-minded thinkers and powerful writers. Although it is now well over half a century since the son followed his father to that heavenly realm into which sin cannot enter, their *doctrine* of sin represented, and still represents, the many who hold to a severely Calvinistic orthodoxy. To my own thinking it is as misleading as it is austere. Take the following statements in *Outlines of Theology*, chapter 21.

"All men . . . are born with an antecedent and prevailing *tendency* in their nature to sin. This innate tendency is itself *sin* in the strictest sense."

But that innate tendency is *not* sin "in the strictest sense", as here said. In the human child let it be viewed, if you will, as an hereditary moral disease, but it certainly is not sin in the sense of *legal default*. An inherited bias is no more sin in a culpable sense than the disease of tuberculosis is a crime, or the thirst for liquor is in itself actual drunkenness. I will not object (as some do) to calling it "sin", for Scripture itself refers to it, at least in the adult, as "sin which dwelleth in me" (Rom. 7: 20), but the excellent Dr. Hodge is surely wrong in asserting that this sin-*inclination* is sin actual. He is equally so when he adds:

"It fully deserves God's wrath and curse." "We begin to exist . . . with a nature which justly condemns us."

Nay, would any man ever be "condemned" even in a human law court for being a *cripple*? Nor is any human being "condemned" by the divine Law for a crippled condition inherited from Adam. To say that it "fully deserves God's *wrath and curse*" is to attribute legal blame to us from babyhood onwards for something involuntary, which we could not escape, and of which we are guiltless. It is something which (according to Hodge) continues to exist *unchanged* in the saints whom God loves, which creates the ironic contradiction that at one and the same time they are both blessed and cursed of God. It is contrary also to various intimations of Scripture; for instance in Genesis 8: 21 God says, "I will *not* again curse the ground for man's sake; for the imagination of man's heart is evil from his youth"— meaning that this inherited depravity, instead of incurring penalty, occasions compassion.

An associated error of this teaching is, that the *guilt* of Adam's transgression is *imputed* to the members of his posterity. Thus Dr. Hodge endorses Quenstedt.

"It was . . . of the highest justice and equity that the sin which Adam, as the root and origin of the whole human race, committed, should be *imputed* to us, and propagated in us so as to constitute us guilty."

But the Bible *nowhere* teaches that Adam's sin is "imputed" to us. It nowhere says that *we* are guilty for what *he* did. "Guilt" is a legal term. There is guilt only where there is actual transgression. Human babes inherit hereditary moral and physical consequences of Adam's fall, but they are not born *guilty!* There simply cannot be guilt until there is transgression. Romans 5: 13 settles that once for all: "Sin is *not* imputed when there is no law" (i.e. where there is no transgression). The point made in Romans 5: 13, 14, is that although sin and death continued between Adam and Moses, yet because the *Law* was not yet given, men were not *transgressors* "after the similitude of Adam", who transgressed a specific command. Mark well that clear distinction which Paul makes: sin and death naturally inherited, but guilt *"not* imputed"!

To my own mind some of the accepted orthodox teachings on this point are intolerable. According to G. F. Wiggers, Augustine's teaching was,

"The *propagation* of Adam's sin among his posterity is a *punishment* of the same sin. The *corruption* of human nature, in the whole race, was the righteous *punishment* of the transgression of the first man."

This makes God Himself the author of sin in Adam's posterity! There is no getting away from that implication if human depravity is viewed as a penal sentence ("punishment") instead of (what it solely is) a *biogenetic* hand-down through racial heredity.

Melancthon's famous *Apology,* or Defence of the Augsburg Confession, even says that as a *penalty* for Adam's sin "human nature was subjected not only to death and corporeal evils, but also *to the reign of the devil.* . . . Defect and concupiscence are both *penal* evils and sins" (italics ours). One wonders which chapter and verse of Scripture can be made to teach such a sickly dogma.

Peter Martyr of Zurich (1500–61) Melancthon's contemporary, says, "Original sin is *inflicted* upon us in *revenge* and punishment of the first fall"; and Calvin's asseveration is tantamount: "God by a just judgment *condemned* us to wrath in Adam, and *willed* us to be *born corrupt* on account of his sin." What libel (although with devout motive) such pronouncements daub across the character of God! What confusion they betray between the forensic and the genetic!—between God's "condemning" and God's *allowing*! between God's judicial will and His *permissive* will! To say, as Calvin does, that God *penally* "willed us to be born corrupt", is not only unscriptural, it is unbearable.

I will not adduce further quotations expressing this traditionally Calvinistic doctrine of "original sin". They all similarly display a harsh exegesis of Romans 5: 12–21, which is the main passage from which such teaching is supposedly extracted. The main appeal is to verse 18: "Therefore as by the offence of one *judgment came* upon all men to condemnation . . ." In the Greek, however, the words, "judgment came" do not occur. But even if we accept the interpolated words, there still remains in this Calvinistic use of Romans 5 a confusion between the Adam race as a whole and individual members of it. Whatever legal "condemnation" fell on the Adam *race* for Adam's sin, fell on it as one undivided *whole* in the judicial *reckoning* of God (not upon individual humans from their very birth) just as when our Lord Jesus died *"all died"* in Him (2 Cor. 5: 14) in the same kind of judicial reckoning.

If the ironcast Calvinist still insists that the first half of Romans 5: 18 means that "by the offence of one judgment came upon all men" *individually*, then the parallel in the second half ("even so, by the righteousness of One, the free gift came upon all men to justification") must mean that all human individuals are now justified, which, however, we know is not the case.

Let this be once-for-all clear in our thinking: none of us inherits Adam's *guilt*: that is his alone. Also, the propensity to sin which I find in my nature is *not* inflicted upon me as a judicial *penalty* for a disobedience committed by someone else six thousand years ago; it is a lamentable but *natural* consequence of human heredity.

But why am I referring to all this? It is because, tied up with it, is a view of our fallen human nature which makes a present inward *sanctification practically impossible*. I turn again to Dr. Alexander Hodge, and find the following didactic definition of sanctification. It seems attractive enough, until we reach the words, "immediately upon death" (which we italicize) and then we suddenly find that real sanctification is postponed until we are the other side of the grave.

"The orthodox doctrine is that the Holy Spirit, by His constant influence upon the whole soul in all its faculties, through the instrumentality of the truth, exercises and develops those holy principles and dispositions which He implanted [in us] in the new birth, until by a constant progress, all sinful dispositions being mortified and extirpated, and all holy dispositions being fully matured, the subject of this grace [i.e. the believer] is brought *immediately upon death* to the measure of the stature of perfect manhood in Christ."

It is a wonderful build-up to a pathetic let-down. Observe the three disqualifying fallacies in it. (1) It postpones full sanctification to the other side of death, whereas the New Testament epistles clearly call us to *entire* sanctification here and now— 1 Thessalonians 5: 23 being a classic representative: "The God of peace Himself *sanctify you wholly*; and may your whole spirit and soul and body be preserved *blameless* unto the coming of our Lord Jesus Christ." (2) It falsely assumes that there is in all Christians "a constant progress" in sanctification, from conversion onwards until death, so that "immediately upon death" it becomes "perfect". Yet all of us know that this "constant progress", lamentably enough, is simply *not true* in thousands of Christians. As plainly as character and conduct can show it, many, instead of becoming increasingly sanctified, become comparatively prayerless, spiritually stationary, sometimes inwardly backslidden, and evidently *less* practically sanctified than they were in the first eager enthusiasms of their Christian life. (3) It ignores the first and simplest meaning of sanctification, which is *set-apartness*, not growth or maturity.

This "orthodox" idea of sanctification holds some awkward problems. Here is a man who dies one year after his conversion. Here is another who lives forty years after his conversion. In order to reach the point where "immediately at death" the "constant progress" of sanctification becomes "perfect", the progress in the first man must be concentrated into one year. But if the necessary progress can be concentrated into one year, why must it be spread out thinly over forty years in the case of the other man who lives longer?

This whole concept of sanctification as a never-complete "progress" up to the time of death is full of strange confusions. There is a strange confusion of the Law of Moses with some supposed law which governed unfallen Adam. Again and again, both in quoting and commenting, Dr. Hodge refers to "the original and absolute law of holiness under which Adam was created"; "the original moral law"; "the original law of God, universal and unchangeable; its demands never can be changed nor compromised. Obedience to this law was the condition of the original covenant of works." In reply to Wesleyan and other holiness teachings according to which God does not require *us*, in our present condition, to keep that original law of holiness, Dr. Hodge argues that although Christ did indeed "satisfy that changeless law in our place", so that we do not have to keep it as the "*condition* of salvation", yet it "does remain our rule of action", to which we must strive to be "*personally* conformed"; for the fulfilling of that law (he says) and *only* that, is true holiness. Yet although we must strive to keep that "original law" of holiness, we simply cannot attain to it (he says) in this present life. He adds, "Perfection is the true aim of the Christian's effort"; yet "in this life" no Christian can "attain a state in which he may live without sin". In other words, we are to keep striving for what we know is utterly impossible.

Such doctrine provokes some big questions. First, what *was* that "original and absolute law of holiness" which supposedly conditioned unfallen Adam? The Bible nowhere speaks of any such. And what *was* that supposed "original covenant of works"? The Bible nowhere speaks of any such. These are mere figments and phantoms of theological theory. The one and only recorded command which God laid upon Adam was that he should not eat from "the tree of the knowledge of good and evil". Whatever else God *may* have required of Adam, there could not have been anything higher, even for that unfallen man, than the twofold precept which was later enunciated through the Law of Moses: "Thou shalt love the Lord thy God with all thy heart, and with all thy soul, and with all thy mind . . . and thou shalt love thy neighbour as thyself."

Further, where do Dr. Hodge and other Calvinists get the strange idea that our Lord Jesus died to save us from the curse of *that* law which supposedly environed unfallen man in Eden? Let me quote: "The *original and absolute* law of God. . . . Christ has been made the end of that law, for (our) righteousness." "Obedience to that law was the condition of the original covenant of works. This condition was broken *by Adam*, but, in our behalf, perfectly fulfilled by Christ." "Christ did . . . satisfy *that changeless law* in our place."

Yet Scripture nowhere says that our Lord died to save us from any such original "law". Its repeated teaching is that He died to do away the curse of the Law of *Moses*. Galatians 3: 13 is representative: "Christ hath redeemed us from the curse of the Law [i.e. of Moses: see 17] being made a curse for us . . . that the blessing of Abraham might come on the Gentiles through Jesus Christ; that we might receive the promise of the Spirit through Faith." And why do the Hodge-type thinkers insist that we Christian believers cannot in our present condition keep that law because we cannot be "perfect"? The Scripture says otherwise. Could anything be clearer than Romans 8: 3, 4?—"For what the Law could not do, in that it was weak through the flesh, God sending His own Son in the likeness of sinful flesh, and [as an offering] for sin, condemned [i.e. passed judgment on] sin in the flesh, that the *requirement* [or ordinance] of the Law might be *fulfilled in us, who walk not after the flesh, but after the Spirit.*"

As for Dr. Hodge's dictum: "Perfection is the true aim of the Christian's effort in every period of growth and in every act," we reply that not one of the seven Greek words which are translated in our New Testament as "perfect", "perfected", "perfecting", "perfection", "perfectly", "perfectness", (60 times altogether)— not one of them in itself means perfection in the absolute sense of faultlessness. Obviously, God cannot and does not expect us, in our present debilitated state, to live as though our human nature were still like that of unfallen Adam. What we now are is by His own permission in the outworking of gracious purpose, so the holiness to which He now calls us is a holiness which is *possible* here and now. There may be a continual inward pervasion by the Holy Spirit, a deep-going renewal of our minds, a true purity throughout our motives, and the very love of God "shed abroad" in our hearts; and that is *a true holiness.*

Dear Christian, whom I now address, I recommend you to reject that teaching on sanctification which we here unfeignedly discountenance, but to which many still adhere today. There may seem to be an impressive, cast iron logic about it when stated by experts like Dr. Hodge, but it is not true to the full New Testament data, and it will drag you about in chains. According to it, we have a sinfulness of nature which cannot be changed in any decisive way this side of heaven; and it sets us striving after an ideal which it tells us we can never attain. The New Testament says that we *can* be "renewed" in the very "spirit of our mind", and that we *can* be "sanctified wholly" here and now, even "blameless" unto the coming again of our Lord Jesus. I say again: that is a true holiness. Our garden *may* be full of fragrant flowers (the positive aspect) even though it is not absolutely without weeds (the negative aspect). No human body on earth is absolutely without disease, yet there may be *abounding health;* and so may it be with the soul. One of the subtlest mistakes of the two Hodges, in my judgment, is their confusing of "entire sanctification", in the Pauline sense, with *sinlessness.*

They are quite right, of course, in referring to their own teaching as the "orthodox" teaching, for it is standardized in the famous Westminster Confession of 1647, along with both the "Larger" and "Smaller" Catechisms which accompanied it. I gratefully associate myself with the many who have lauded that Confession and those Catechisms as a monumental synopsis of Biblical doctrine; but I cannot concede that without exception the propositions therein are truly Scriptural. If we want to be convinced that practical sanctification is a pathetic impossibility in this present life, all we need to do is consult the answer to Question 149 in the Larger Catechism (note the words which we here italicize):

"No man is able, either of himself, *or by any grace received* in this life, perfectly to *keep the commandments* of God; but doth daily break them in thought, word, and deed."

Such is the dismal dogma; but is it truly Scriptural? What about Zacharias and Elizabeth (Luke 1: 6), "righteous before

God, walking in *all the commandments* of the Lord, *blameless*"? What about Colossians 4: 12, "That ye may stand *perfect* and *complete* in *all* the will of God"? What about Hebrews 13: 21, "make you *perfect* in every good work to do His will"?—not to mention half a dozen other such references. Or what about Romans 13: 10, "*Love* is the *fulfilling* of the *law*"?—or Ephesians 1: 4, "holy and *without blame* before Him, in love"—and others?

With good reason the late President Asa Mahan of Oberlin made the following comments: "Let us now contemplate the iron bands of [this] theological dogma; bands which render the normal growth of the born-anew soul as impossible as did the cruel bands which bound the feet of female infants among the Chinese. Take two or three of these dogmas as examples: 'No man is able, either of himself or by any grace received in this life, perfectly to keep the commandments of God, but daily doth break them in thought, word, and deed.' Thus the convert is started on his course with a professed revelation from God, that he has no power, either of himself or from any grace vouchsafed in this life, to render the obedience required of him, and that, as a matter of fact, every day of his life he will break these requirements 'in thought, word, and deed.'

"But what, according to these dogmas, is the state of the believer when he *does* sin? Listen to the answer: 'True believers, by reason of the unchangeable love of God and his decree and covenant to give them perseverance . . . can neither totally nor finally fall away from the state of grace.' . . . 'Nevertheless they may, through the temptations of Satan and the world, the prevalency of corruption remaining in them, and the neglect of the means of their preservation, fall into grievous sins, and for a time continue therein; whereby they incur God's displeasure, and grieve His Holy Spirit, and come to be deprived of some measure of their graces and comforts, have their hearts hardened, and their consciences wounded, hurt and scandalize others, and bring temporal judgments upon themselves.' (Westminster Confession, chapter 19, article 3).

"Thus the young convert is taught that he cannot receive grace sufficient fully to obey God, but must daily sin in thought, word, and deed, yet he has a divine assurance that, however he sins, he will not utterly fall away from God. . . . What could God do more, to insure in every born-anew soul a back-sliding life, than to require of it an absolute belief that it will sin 'daily in thought, word, and deed', but that no form or degree of sin it can commit will imperil its immortal interests?"

As already noted, there is a subtle confusion of holiness or sanctification with faultlessness or sinlessness. Take a final quotation, this time from Dr. *Charles* Hodge. The italics in the quotation are our own.

"The thing to be done is to turn from sin to holiness ; to love God perfectly and our neighbour as ourselves ; to perform every duty without *defect* or *omission,* and keep *ourselves* from all sin of thought, word, or deed, of heart or life. Can any man do this? Does any man need argument to convince him that he cannot do it? He knows . . . that he can no more do this than he can raise the dead."

Surely the confusion scarcely needs pointing out. Our love to God supposedly has to be "perfect" in the sense of nothing less than a faultless emotion or moral capability. Despite all the badly broken strings, the piano must play a note-perfect melody. Every "duty" down to the minutest tremors of moral consciousness must be fulfilled "without *defect* or *omission*", in "thought, word, deed, heart, life". But who *says* that God calls us to such faultlessness in this present life? Charles Hodge may, but the Bible does *not*. As already mentioned, none of the several Greek words translated as "perfect" in our New Testament means perfection in the absolute sense.

Oddly enough, having set the demand impossibly high, Dr. Hodge makes the means impossibly low, i.e. we are to "keep *ourselves* from all sin". How thoroughly we agree with him that none of us can! But how different is the New Testament teaching, that we may be a very "habitation of God through the Spirit" (Eph. 2: 22), "strengthened with might by His Spirit in the inner man" (3: 16), "filled unto all the fulness of God" (3: 19), "transformed by the *renewing* of our *mind*" (Rom. 12: 2), and that we may have God Himself "working *in* us", a "completeness in *every* good work to do His will" (Heb. 13: 21)!

To sum up: Calvinism as represented by the Westminster Confession and others tells us in effect: Sanctification is moral perfection, nothing less, and therefore "sanctification can never be perfected in this life" (Hodge: vol. 3, p. 245); yet although perfect sanctification is impossible in this life, that is what we are constantly to strive after, because "the divine law . . . condemns as *sinful* any lack of conformity to the standard of absolute perfection" (ibid. 246). Could anything be more tantalizing?

What strange self-contradictions such doctrine involves! It creates the unthinkable paradox that Adam was imperfect even before the Fall. Did unfallen Adam's love for God have the required *"absolute perfection"*? If it did, why did Adam wilfully *disobey* God?

It hardly fits, to blame Adam's free-will, for an "absolute perfection" of love would have kept his free-will from disobeying. Nor is it any answer to say that Adam disobeyed because he was deceived, for how could an "absolute perfection" of moral and mental condition be deceived? And besides, although Eve *was* beguiled, Adam was *not*. He was not even tempted. That is why Paul writes, "Adam was not deceived, but the woman being deceived was in the transgression" (1 Tim. 2: 14). Adam disobeyed knowingly and deliberately. As Genesis 3: 17 says, he "hearkened unto the voice of his wife", and disobeyed because he chose to remain one with *her* in preference to remaining true to God without her. How, then, did he love God with an "absolute perfection" of love in "heart and soul and strength"?

But now let me point to one of Adam's fallen posterity, a "sinful man", who seemingly loved God more than Adam did. He longed and prayed for a son, year after year, but his precious wife could not become a mother. Then, by a lovely miracle, when he was one hundred years old, and his wife ninety, the beautiful baby boy, Isaac, was born to them. Can any of us imagine vividly enough how inexpressibly precious that handsome young son was to them? Yet just as he was developing from youth to young manhood, God said to Abraham, "Take now thy son, *thine only Isaac* whom thou *lovest* . . . and offer him for a burnt offering". Without a hint of demur, though his mind must have been staggered, Abraham proceeded to obey. He built the altar, bound his beloved Isaac upon it, and lifted the knife. Whose love for God was the greater?—unfallen Adam's, or Abraham's? I make bold to say that unfallen Adam never loved God like that.

We may carry this a bit further. Whose *mind* was truer to God?—unfallen Adam's or young Joseph's? Adam sinned without any need and without any provocation, whereas Joseph, under pressure of seductive solicitation, *refused* to grieve God, crying out, "How *can* I do this, and sin against God?" Perhaps the apostle John had that in mind when he wrote, "Whosoever is begotten of God doth not commit sin, for his seed abideth in him [i.e. his regenerate new life] and he *cannot* sin, because he is born of God". John means, not that sin has become either mentally or physically impossible to the born-again man, but that the born-again man "cannot" in the sense that it has become morally intolerable.

So, then, whose love meant more to God?—unfallen Adam's, or Abraham's? Whose integrity was the more "perfect"?—unfallen Adam's, giving way without solicitation, or virtuous Joseph's, too strong for the subtlest wiles of the flesh? These things give many of us good reason to rethink this whole matter of sanctification. The Calvinistic authorities to which we have referred surely use that word "perfect" ambiguously, as also that expression, "absolute perfection". Can we *ever* use that word "absolute" of *any* moral condition outside of God Himself? For my own part, I believe that all moral "perfection" outside of God Himself is relative, and can *only* be so.

Why this continual harking back to Adam? For, as we all know, we cannot now have a perfect bodily organism, or a perfect mental mechanism, such as *he* had ; but we *can* love God just as much as he did—maybe *more,* as the redeemed, regenerated "sons of God" in Christ, with an adoring gratitude which unfallen Adam never knew. Also, we *can* have a guileless integrity like that of Joseph's, which apparently was stronger than that of Adam's! Think of it: not one virtue of unfallen Adam is preserved for us, either to admire or to emulate. Yes, there was utter sinlessness before the Fall ; but sinlessness is negative. Was there positive *holiness*? I do not deny ; I only ask ; but so far as all the available data go, both in the Genesis account and in all subsequent Scripture reference, there is only the negative ; nor is unfallen Adam ever once held up as a moral example.

As for that supposed "original and absolute law of holiness" under which Adam is assumed to have been probatively placed, nowhere (as we have already observed) does Scripture disclose any such. But whatever law, either revealed or unrevealed, Adam may have been under, in addition to the command not to eat of the forbidden tree, he simply could not have rendered a truer fulfilling of its commands than that which 1 Timothy 1: 5 declares is possible to ourselves, i.e. "Now the end [i.e. goal, or ultimate] of the command [or charge] is *LOVE OUT OF A PURE HEART.*" Could even unfallen Adam render more than that? We are all needing to see afresh (especially many Calvinist thinkers) that fundamentally sin is a matter, not of the will only, or even of desire, but of *motive*; so is holiness, whether in unfallen or fallen man. Not even the many constitutional defects which I inherit in Adam exclude the possibility of thoroughly cleansed and sublimated motives within me when once the Holy Spirit has regenerated me, and "renewed" me, and infilled me, and thus sanctified me. If we want to see how far Calvinist dogmatics have strayed from this and from Scripture, we only need to place side by side a statement by a scholarly representative and one from the apostle Paul:

"The doctrine of Lutherans and Reformed, the two great branches of the Protestant Church, is, that *sanctification is never perfected in this life*" (*Systematic Theology*, vol. 3, p. 245).	"The very God of peace *sanctify you wholly*; and your whole *spirit* and *soul* and *body* be preserved *blameless* unto the coming of our Lord Jesus Christ" (I Thess. 5: 23).

So, according to traditional Calvinism we *cannot* be completely sanctified in this present life, but according to Paul we *can*, and he prays that we *may* be. What, then, is our verdict? Is not this a case where some of us must choose between venerated orthodoxy and plain Scripture? My own advice is: Hold firmly to the Word itself rather than to any traditional interpretation which smothers it. I counsel you to reject the gloomy blunder that there cannot be on earth a thorough renewal of our moral nature into true holiness. Let us believe the divine promise that "entire sanctification" is provided for us *now*, in Christ.

> Yes, I believe Thee, Lord divine,
> That holiness may now be mine ;
> That Thou canst remedy within
> These inborn aptitudes to sin ;
> That every motive, thought, desire,
> May be refined in Thy pure fire ;
> That all my mind may be renewed,
> And by Thy Spirit fresh-endued :
> Come, gracious Lord, in me begin
> This renovation deep within ;
> Transfuse within me, even here,
> The holy love which casts out fear.
> So shall Thy grace be magnified
> Through me, "a vessel sanctified",
> And thus shall I in measure know
> The joy of heaven on earth below.

SANCTIFICATION AND HEREDITY

Verily, there is nothing so true, that the damps of error
have not warped it;
Verily, there is nothing so false, that a sparkle of truth
is not in it.
For the enemy, the father of lies, the giant Upas of
creation,
Whose deadly shade hath blasted this once green garden
of the Lord,
Can but pervert the good, but may not create the evil;
He destroyeth, but cannot build; for he is not another
deity:
Mighty is his stolen power, yet is he a creature and a
subject;
Not a maker of abstract wrong, but a spoiler of concrete
right:
The fiend hath not a royal crown; he is but a prowling
robber,
Suffered, for some mysterious end, to haunt the King's
highway;
And the keen sword he beareth, once was a simple
ploughshare;
Yea, and his panoply of error is but a distortion of the
truth:
The sickle that once reaped righteousness, beaten from
its useful curve,
With axe, and spike, and bar, headeth the marauder's
halbert.
Seek not further, O man, to solve the dark riddle of sin;
Suffice it, that thine own bad heart is to thee thine origin
of evil.

Martin F. Tupper's
Proverbial Philosophy.

SANCTIFICATION AND HEREDITY

IN OUR reflections on sanctification according to orthodox Calvinism we encountered what I can only call the deadly dogma that the very *guilt* of Adam is imputed to all his posterity, the fearful concomitant of which is, that thousands of millions have been divinely predestined to a never-ending damnation through a transgression of which they are innocent. Let those boast such Calvinism who will; as for myself, it contradicts all that is most natively human in me.

I know that such teaching can be set forth with seemingly compelling logic, especially by masters of theological polemics like those two former Princeton giants, Charles and Alexander Hodge. Yet ironically enough I find myself protesting in the very words used by Charles Hodge himself against Finney: "a remarkable product of relentless logic . . . conclusions which are indeed logical deductions, but which shock the moral sense, and prove nothing but that the premises are false."

However, while I deny the Scripturalness of the supposition that Adam's *guilt* is imputed to his descendants, I am equally sure that Calvinism is soundly Scriptural in teaching hereditary *sin-infection* from Adam throughout the race. We are sinners, not only through our own volitional malfunctioning, but by a communicated moral perversion which we inherited at our birth, as members of Adam's fallen race. In this there is nothing judicial or penal: it is a permitted natural consequence of racial unity and heredity. The traditional theological name for that transmitted malady is "original sin", though it is far from the best phrase to hang on it.

You whom I now address are not the kind to be gulled by modern evolutionary speculations which treat sin as an interim peculiarity in the "upward march" of mankind. Nor, if we believe the Bible, will any of us give credence to the "new psychology" equivocation that sin is merely "the under-side of the good", or that moral evil is merely a matter of relativity. But when some outstanding Evangelical leader or school ably propounds an erroneous view of "original sin" or of heredity, in a system of teaching which otherwise is excellent, then even Bible-believing Christians can be in danger. One thing will be clear to all of us: a defective view of heredity must always certainly lead to a wrong doctrine of *sanctification*. That is what we are concerned with here.

ORIGINAL SIN DENIED

Ever since the monk Pelagius, in the early fifth century, there have been periodic denials of "original sin". Pelagius and his disciples, Caelestius and Julian of Eclanum, taught that there was no such thing as an inherited sin-bias in human nature. All who are born into this world are the same in moral nature as Adam before the Fall. Instead of a sin-ward imbalance there is an absolute equipoise of the will.

Perhaps the most powerful pen against "original sin" in recent times was that of Charles G. Finney who died in 1875, but whose monumental work, *Systematic Theology*, still powerfully speaks for him in many an evangelical minister's study. What Finney *was* greatly augments the wide influence of what he taught. Undoubtedly in the "holy war" he was a "mighty man of valour". Never was there a more dynamic evangelist, and certainly never one whose itinerations were more consistently accompanied by supernatural visitations. He was famous by what he wrought as a preacher before ever he became famous by what he taught as a tutor. As an evangelist he was a veritable Elijah (greatest of the *preaching* prophets). At Oberlin he became their Isaiah (greatest of the *writing* prophets). Both by voice and pen he was a Christian leader of great stature. It was that which made his teaching against "original sin" seem the more trustable.

In that peculiarity, however, he was surely wrong; and, with his large volume now lying before me, I counsel all who would know what a truly Scriptural sanctification is to reject the denial of "original sin". If we accept such arguments as Finney's against "original sin" we are easily lured into false ideas of sanctification such as his own well-meant but erroneous doctrine of *perfectionism*, i.e. that sanctification is sinlessness. Let no one think that the consideration which we here devote to his teaching is tedious or out-of-date. I frequently meet people (some of whom know little about Finney himself) who have been side-tracked into delusion by hand-down of his theory. What, then, are Finney's main arguments against "original sin"?

On pages 249 and 250 of his *Systematic Theology* we find the centre-point around which the whole scheme of his thinking revolves. He claims that sin cannot be an inhering quality of the soul because sin consists entirely in an *activity* of the *will*. In other words, sin is something which I *do*, not something which I *am*. Here is his own statement:

"We deny that the human constitution is morally depraved, because it is impossible that sin should be a quality of the *substance* of soul or body. Sin is, and must be, a quality of *choice* or intention, and not of substance."

That is an outright denial of all hereditary sin-bias; but Finney thinks he has Scriptural reason for it, as his further words explain:

"To make sin an attribute or quality of *substance* is contrary to *God's* definition of sin. 'Sin,' says the apostle, is *anomia*, a 'transgression' of, or want of conformity to, the moral law. That is, it consists in a refusal to love God and our neighbour, or, which is the same thing, in loving ourselves supremely."

The big fault here is that Finney blinks all those Scripture passages where the word, "sin", is used to describe, not only an activity, but a *proclivity*. One such is Romans 7. "The evil that I would not do, that I do. Now if I do that which I would not, it is no more I that do it, but *sin that dwelleth in me*." Paul's words indicate a disorder deeper down and further back than the *will*; a strange disorder issuing in active evil *despite* the will to do otherwise. Finney may refuse to call it sin because in itself it is not actual transgression, but that does not alter the fact that the inherited disposition is *there*, nor does it rub out those places where Scripture *calls* it "sin".

The fact is, Finney's definition of sin as being solely "transgression" is not really a definition of sin at all, but only of *sinning*. Paul distinctly tells us, in Romans 5: 12–14, that even between Adam and Moses, when there was *no* "transgression" of the Law (because the Law was not yet given) "*sin* was in the world" (i.e. sinfulness both in condition and in conduct). However, Finney now presents a further argument:

"To represent the [human] constitution as sinful is to represent God, who is the author of the constitution, as the author of sin. To say that God is not the direct former of the constitution, but that sin is conveyed by natural generation from Adam who made himself sinful is only to remove the objection one step further back, not to obviate it; for God established the physical laws which of necessity bring about this result."

Such reasoning ill becomes a Finney. It is tantamount to arguing that because God allowed Lucifer to turn himself into the devil through wrong exercise of free-will, God is the author of sin; or that because God permitted the Jewish leaders to crucify Christ, God Himself is the real perpetrator of the Crucifixion. But now comes a third arrow from the stalwart's quiver:

"How came Adam by a sinful nature? Did his first sin *change* his nature? Or did God change it as a *penalty* for sin? What ground is there for the assertion that Adam's nature became in itself sinful by the Fall? This is a groundless, not to say ridiculous, assumption, and an absurdity. Sin an attribute of nature! Sin a substance! Is it a solid, a fluid, a material, or a spiritual substance?"

Finney's over-confidence here cannot hide his strange ignoring of plain Scripture, that the Fall *did* bring a chronic change in Adam's nature. Hitherto there had been joyful fellowship with God, but now Adam and Eve, instead of eagerly hasting to Him as before, slink away, and hide from Him *"afraid"*. Instead of communion there is now fear and alienation. Instead of innocence they now "know good *and evil*". Their "eyes are opened" (i.e. their inward eyes). Nakedness must now be covered, for from now onward they are a danger to each other. Strange new susceptibilities have suddenly awakened. Also, they must now be expelled from that paradise, and debarred by a "flaming sword", lest they get to the "tree of life". All this *does* indicate a serious inward change, especially so in the light of Paul's comment in Romans 5: 12, "By one man *sin* entered into the world". Paul certainly did not mean merely that by the one man *"transgression"* entered into the world; for if (as Finney argues) Adam's children are all born sinless, then "transgression" enters fresh into the world by millions, not just "by one man".

But Finney presses his case still further. Not only does he reduce sin to no more than a wrong activity of the will, he denies that the will itself is depraved. He says, "Moral depravity is the depravity of free-will, not of the faculty itself, but only of its free action". In other words, depravity is only functional not constitutional. What he nowhere satisfactorily explains, however, is *why* the will (which is only the executive of desire, not the originator) so malfunctions. How *can* there be continuous wrong volition unless there is some wrong activation in the *nature*? If Finney's idea is right, then even the devil does not have moral depravity in himself; his trouble is not sinful motive, but only a faulty mechanism.

Next, on page 231, Finney says that moral depravity "cannot consist in anything back of choice". What, then, about sinful *desires* which lie behind choice? Are not *they* moral depravity? No, says Finney, because they are never desires for sin as such, but only for what gratifies the self. When Eve desired the forbidden fruit it was not a craving for *sin* but for something "pleasant to the eyes" and "to make one wise". Agreed, but when Finney makes that his basis for saying, "All men sin in precisely the same way", he is miles astray. What about Cain's fratricide soon afterward? Did *that* spring from a purely non-moral desire? Was there not jealousy and hate? And are not *they* sinful emotions or predispositions?

Finney is utterly wrong in saying that whatever lies behind choice is non-moral because involuntary. Every desire for something which is *known* to be sinful is *sinful desire*, even though its urge may be for self-gratification. Cain's desire to kill Abel was itself sinful before ever there was "choice" or "will" or "act". Similarly, *every* desire for what is *known* to be evil is evil desire. Finney may refuse to call it "moral depravity" or "sin", but at that point Finney and Scripture part company. Indeed our Lord Himself says that lecherous *desire* is sin in heart even where there is no immoral act; also that unprovoked anger is sin even though it does not physically smite (Matt. 5: 22, 28). Finney says that those involuntary states are *not* sin, or "moral depravity". Our Lord says they *are*.

But now, finally, if (as Finney avers) there is no hereditary sin-bent, how does he explain the continuous *universality* of sin? He says it is because our inborn "sensibilities" mislead the will from birth onwards.

"Sensibility acts as a powerful impulse to the will from the moment of birth, and secures the consent and activity of the will to procure its gratification, before *reason* is at all developed. . . . This committed *state* of the will is not moral depravity, and has no moral character until a sense of moral obligation is developed. The moment this [i.e. our awaking to moral consciousness] is developed, this committal of the will to self-indulgence must be abandoned, or it *becomes* moral depravity. But as the will is already in a *state* of committal, and has to some extent already formed the habit of seeking to gratify feeling . . . the will *retains its hold* on self-gratification. . . . This selfish choice is the wicked heart—the propensity to sin—which causes what is generally termed actual transgression. This sinful choice is properly called indwelling sin. It is the latent, standing, controlling preference of the mind." (Italics ours.)

Finney's self-refutation here is bold. He says that from birth innate "sensibility" captures the will for self-gratification; then he slips into the very reverse and says it is the *will* which "retains *its* hold on self-gratification"! Which, then, is it? The answer is: Neither, because Finney ignores what is deeper than either "sensibility" or "will", namely, inborn *desire*.

Again if, according to Finney, it is "ridiculous" to say that Adam's sin "changed his nature", how can he now say that this "self-gratification" *does* change the nature in all Adam's children? He says it produces a "wicked heart", a "propensity to sin", a "controlling preference of the mind", all of which are *qualities*, ingrained characteristics, not just a poise of the will. In reality, Finney has now rebutted his own dictum, that "moral depravity" is only in "volition" (function) and not in "substance" (nature), and that sin is *only* "transgression".

His attempted explanation leaves untouched the stubborn mystery of inborn *predisposition*—for instance juvenile desire to inflict pain on an animal while the child is still in the period Finney describes as "before reason is developed". During that period, so he says, there cannot be moral depravity, but only "gratification of the *self*". But (we reply) if that "self" urges gratification through what is intrinsically cruel, then plainly the "self" is originally corrupt. Other such early dispositions—deceit, stealing, and so on, all denote the same thing.

Finney's case gets weaker the more we pry it open. He is obliged to admit that we everywhere see hereditary defects transmitted through human *physical* nature (form, features, etc.), and through our *mental* nature (aptitudes, tempers, etc.); yet he denies that there is any such transmission in our *moral* nature; surely a strange inconsistency.

Moreover, he has to admit that the universal temptation which causes universal sin arises from *within our nature itself*: "The human sensibility is, manifestly, deeply depraved"! He even says, "The representations of Scripture are, that the *body* is the occasion of sin"—which strongly savours of the Gnostic error that matter itself is evil.

And yet again, in denying that the universality of sin proves "*original* sin", he asks, "If sin necessarily implies a sinful *nature*, how did Adam and Eve sin? Had *they* a sinful nature? How did angels sin? Had *they* a sinful nature?" The fact is, that the vast majority of the angel myriads did *not* sin; therefore no conclusion about *all* can be drawn from only *some*; but in the case of our human race, if there is not "original sin" why is it that among all the billions born from Adam downwards there has not been *one* without sin?—except, of course, our Lord Jesus, whose birth was immaculate.

Could anything be more self-contradictory than the following paragraph? Note carefully the words which we italicize.

"Why is sin so natural to mankind? Not because their nature is itself sinful, but because the *appetites* and passions *tend* so strongly to self-indulgence. These are *temptations to sin*, but sin itself consists not in these appetites and *propensities*, but in the voluntary committal of the will to their indulgence" (257).

So the "nature itself" is not "sinful", yet its innate "appetites" are "*temptations* to sin". But how *can* they be so, unless innately perverse? If the very propensities of the new-born self lead to sin, then there is indeed "original sin".

SANCTIFICATION: A WRONG WAY

Here, of course, our special interest in this denial of "original sin" is its bearing upon our subject, *sanctification*. Eighty pages are devoted to this in Finney's *Systematic Theology*, but the following few excerpts are sufficient to show his main idea.

"Holiness consists, not at all in the *constitution* of body or mind; but it belongs, strictly, only to the *will* or heart, and consists in *obedience of will* to the law of God, as it lies revealed in the intellect. It is expressed in one word, love; this love is identical with the entire consecration of the whole being to the glory of God." (p. 403, italics ours.)

Observe here the ambiguous equation of "will" and "heart"; holiness belongs "only to the will or heart". That is a confusion. Both in Scripture and in common usage "heart" means the human "self". There are 958 occurrences of "heart" in our King James Version; and almost invariably when used in its figurative sense, it represents either the whole mental and moral being, or the centre-point of thought, desire, feeling. On page 411 Finney actually *says* that the "heart" is the *soul*.

Yet elsewhere Finney *denies* that there can be sanctification of heart and soul. In the foregoing quotation he says that sanctification consists "in *obedience of will* to the law of God". In another place (405) he says, "Sanctification, then, is nothing more nor less than entire *obedience,* for the time being, to the moral law". In other words, when our will is fully obeying the moral law we are sanctified, for sanctification is not an interior state, but an activity of the will.

What then is *entire* sanctification? Finney's limping "explanation" is that it means no more than *continuous* obedience. To quote his own words on page 452, it is "entire, in the sense of *perpetual* sanctification". Or, more fully, "Sanctification may be entire in two senses: (1) in the sense of present, *full obedience,* or entire consecration to God; and (2) in the sense of *continued* consecration or obedience to God". So even *entire* sanctification, according to Finney, does not extend beyond the will: it is full and continuing obedience or yieldedness ("consecration"). There is *no* renewal of heart, mind, soul, nature. He says: "Sanctification does *not* imply any constitutional change, either of soul or body"(404). It consists in an *act* of the will, which becomes a *set* of the will, then a *state* of the will; but nothing more (405).

So, in sanctification, according to Finney, the big thing is somehow to get the will *"established"* in obedience; and (I gather) intense was the effort, agonizing the struggle, exhausting the repeated failure, and pathetic the eventual recoil of Finney's disciples who prayed and groaned and wept and strained to "establish" or "confirm" their will in utter obedience, minute by minute, to "the law of God as revealed in the intellect". Poor souls! Some of them, it would seem, suffered shipwreck of faith through it. Sad irony, that Finney of all men, the fiery Elijah who himself had such transforming experience of God, should so misteach it in the attempt to give it dogmatic expression!

A cardinal error is his concept of the will as "the *controlling faculty* of the mind", which it certainly is not. The will is the executant only, not the originator of thought and desire. *Behind* the will is impulse, thought, desire, motive, urge. Because that is so, the big refutation of Finney's theory is the stubborn fact of human *consciousness*. Universal experience is that you cannot make the will act morally right when the heart behind it is morally wrong. Also, the more truly we penetrate our human consciousness to its first glimmerings in infancy, so the more do we confirm that the sin-bias in our nature is *not* something which we merely *acquire* on reaching years of so-called "discretion". Nay, there was a prior disposition which *caused* later transgression. Does not the phenomenon that every duck takes to water as soon as it is hatched, prove that by its nature it is an aquatic fowl? And does it not prove something by parallel, that we human beings, without exception, from our earliest moral beginnings, show proneness to wrong despite all protest of hereditary good within us?

Another cardinal error of Finney is his confusing of holiness with *sinlessness*. He says, "It is nonsense to speak of a holiness that consists with sin". "Entire sanctification consists in *perfect* obedience to the law of God." "Nothing is holiness short of full obedience to the moral law." At a glance, such statements may *seem* to be true, but they are not so. There *can* be holiness of *motive* even though there remain cross-currents of wrong urge in the nature. Indeed, such holiness of motive is the more commendably holy because it *overcomes* all temptation to the contrary. Not flawless legal perfection, but thorough purity of *motive* is the holiness to which God now calls us; not faultlessness but *blamelessness* (Eph. 1: 4).

Finney's teaching on sanctification issued in what became known as the *"alternation"* theory of sanctification. Note the italicized words in the following quotation: "Sanctification, then, is nothing more or less than entire obedience, *for the time being, to the moral law."* This means that there can be one moment of "entire obedience", (i.e. entire sanctification) followed immediately by a moment of *defective* conformity, (i.e. *de*-sanctification). That is because sanctification (according to Finney) consists exclusively in *will*-conformity to the moral law. It is not an inward state, but a suspense or poise of volition. By turns, a hundred times a day, one may be *all*-sanctified and *non*-sanctified. By a momentary lapse we are altogether *un*sanctified; by another moment of contrition and return to obedience we are *re-sanctified*. Hence the emphasis on getting an "established" will, and a "permanent" self-consecration.

Dr. Asa Mahan, Finney's colleague at Oberlin, thus refers to this tantalizing concept of sanctification.

"No individual, I believe, ever disciplined believers so severely and with such intense and tireless patience as my Brother Finney. . . . His most earnest efforts were put forth to induce among believers *permanence* in the divine life. In accomplishing this he knew of but one method: absolute and fixed renunciation of sin, consecration to God, and purpose of obedience.

"When he came to Oberlin, and entered upon the duties of his Professorship, he felt that God had given him a blessed opportunity to realize in perfection his ideal of a ministry for the churches. He had before him a mass of talented and promising theological students, who had implicit confidence in the wisdom of their teacher, and with equal sincerity would follow his instructions and admonitions. Accordingly, for months in succession, he gathered together those students at stated seasons, instructed them most carefully in regard to the nature of the *renunciation of sin, consecration to Christ* and *purpose of obedience,* required of them. Then, under his teachings and admonitions, they would renew their *renunciations, consecrations* and *purposes of obedience,* with all the intensity and fixedness of resolve of which their natures were capable. The result, in every case, was one and the same: not the new life of joy and peace and power which was anticipated, but groaning bondage under the law of sin and death."

Oh, let me urge the following recommendations upon all whose heart-longing is to live in the experience of entire sanctification. Stay with the Bible doctrine of original sin, or hereditary sin-proclivity; for to imagine a false immunity from that inherited condition prevents any of us from understanding how sanctification in Christ *deals* with it. Stay with the New Testament doctrine that true sanctification really *does* something deep down in our moral nature, breaking the power of inherited depravity by a thorough "renewing" of the mind.

Yes, stay with that New Testament doctrine, for it is God's own answer to a pained heart-cry which we find in the *Old* Testament. Remember: the same David who groaned, "Behold, I was shapen in iniquity" (Ps. 51: 5) was inspired to pray (verse 10), "CREATE IN ME A CLEAN HEART, O GOD, AND RENEW A RIGHT SPIRIT WITHIN ME".

Sanctification and Depravity

Error is a hardy plant; it flourisheth in every soil;
In the heart of the wise and good, alike with the wicked
and foolish.
For there is no error so crooked, but it hath in it some
lines of truth:
Nor is any poison so deadly, that it serveth not some
wholesome use:
And the just man, enamoured of the right, is blinded by
the speciousness of wrong;
And the prudent, perceiving an advantage, is content to
overlook the harm.
On all things created remaineth the half-effaced signature
of God,
Somewhat of fair and good, though blotted by the finger
of corruption:
And if error cometh in like a flood, it mixeth with
streams of truth;
And the Adversary loveth to have it so, for thereby
many are decoyed.
Providence is dark in its permissions; yet one day, when
all is known,
The universe of reason shall acknowledge how just and
good were they;

Martin F. Tupper's
Proverbial Philosophy.

SANCTIFICATION AND DEPRAVITY

PERHAPS the last two studies in this present series may have seemed tedious to some of us who are more eager to concentrate on the *positive* possibilities of sanctification. Yet most of us need not only to be guided into the sure path of truth, but *guarded* against byways or error, especially so since some of these latter look like well-paved highways.

We know what happened when that evangelical warrior, Charles G. Finney, became carried away with a new brand of Pelagianism which denies "original sin". His name meant so much to so many that a multitude of enthusiasts followed him into a delusive doctrine of sanctification which eventually left them stranded in bewilderment.

But besides *denial* of "original sin" there can be an equally wrong *overstating* of it; and it is that which claims our attention here. There is a theory of hereditary depravity which renders sanctification hopeless. Moreover, it comes to us under such an aegis of venerated names and with such a sacrosanctity of tradition that one is made to feel impertinent in challenging it. Yet it misrepresents Scripture; it debars numberless Christians from the sunlit Canaan of entire sanctification; and its melancholy exaggerations of human depravity deserve severe castigation.

Not long ago a minister in a rural area preached a sermon on "Total Depravity". Afterwards a farmer said, "Preacher, that total depravity's a fine doctrine, if only we could all live up to it". The *Westminster Confession,* one of the great documents which have moulded Protestant belief in Britain and America, especially among Presbyterians, certainly seems determined that we shall all "live up to it". Its teaching turns experiential sanctification into mere wishful thinking. Take the following solemn declarations from chapter 6, articles 2, 4, 5 and 6. Ponder particularly the words which we italicize.

"By this sin they ['our first parents'] fell from their original righteousness and communion with God, and so became dead in sin, and *wholly defiled in all the faculties and parts of soul and body."*

"From this original corruption, whereby we are utterly indisposed, disabled, and *made opposite to all good, and wholly inclined to all evil*, do proceed all actual transgressions."

"This corruption of nature, during this life, doth *remain* in those that are regenerated: and although it be through Christ pardoned and mortified, yet both itself and *all* the motions thereof are truly and properly *sin*."

"Every sin, both *original* and actual, being a *transgression* of the righteous law of God, and contrary thereto, doth, in its own nature, bring *guilt* upon the sinner, whereby he is bound over to the wrath of God, and curse of the law, and *so* made subject to death, with all miseries spiritual, temporal, *eternal*."

Who is to be charged with disrespect for wondering how such scholarly men as those Westminster divines could formulate such grim dogmatic extravaganzas? Not one of their accompanying Scripture texts warrants such extreme pronouncements.

Think of it: *"wholly* defiled in *all* the faculties and parts of *soul* and *body*!"* If that were true, men would be demons, not humans, and earth would already be hell. If it were true, not even regeneration, let alone sanctification, would be possible. But it is *not* true. It is belied by the persistence and frequent prevalence of goodness on earth in both B.C. and A.D. eras of history; in both Christian and non-Christian areas. I say "goodness", and I *mean* goodness; not *perfect* goodness (for in that sense, as our Lord said, "There is none good save One, even God"). I mean genuine human goodness of motive, purpose, desire, ideal, and activity, *along* with and *despite* all the hereditary evils which continually war against it but can no more conquer it than they can be conquered *by* it in the present state of things.

Yes, as surely as the Bible is true, there is hereditary *good* as well as hereditary evil. If heredity had transmitted only evil, and dammed off all good at each new procreation, the Adam race would by now have become self-exterminated, or history a terrestrial inferno.

It is a mistake to think (as some evidently do) that the more we vilify man, the more we glorify God. We are not being irreverent, but only true to what Scripture teaches, when we reflect that God Himself is responsible for both man and heredity. We should go the whole way with Biblical teaching on human depravity, but not beyond it. If we force Scripture to mean something unwarrantably *worse* than it actually testifies we not only thereby misappreciate the remedy which God has provided in the Gospel, but we libel God Himself who foresaw and permitted such an unmitigable degradation.

That theological phrase, "total depravity", needs using with discrimination. Strictly, the word, "depravity", refers to the mental and moral, not the physical. By "total" depravity is meant that every part of man's mental and moral nature is vitiated in greater or lesser degree. In that sense the depravity *must* be "total", for all those mysterious intangibles of man's spiritual nature, i.e. intellect, volition, emotion, intelligence, instinct, desire, motive, urge, disposition, tempers, not only live inseparably *with* each other, they live *within* each other, all *together* constituting one, indivisible, thinking mind. A disease of any is necessarily a disease of the whole exquisitely integrated, self-conscious entity. Yet although "total" means that *all* the "parts" (for want of a better word) are affected, it does not mean that *all* the parts are *all* bad.

We may make a parallel with the human body. There is no human body on earth which is absolutely free from disease. From birth, every part is affected in greater or lesser degree by that hereditary infection which eventually issues in death. Yet though all parts are affected, it is utterly untrue to say that *all* the parts are *all* disease. Degrees of disease, latent, dormant, chronic, may coexist with degrees of *health* in the same body. Along with hereditary mortality there can be inherited *vitality*.

Hereditary moral evil, alas, there undoubtedly is in plenty throughout the human race. Its ugliness leers at us continually all round the world, while without respite it plagues our own hearts. To deny hereditary depravity is to bang our heads against a Gibraltar of contrary evidence as well as to disbelieve the testimony of Scripture. Yet it is just as wrong to deny hereditary goodness as to deny hereditary evil. The Westminster Confession is untrue when it avers that through original corruption we are "*utterly* indisposed, disabled, and made *opposite to all good, and wholly inclined to all evil*".

Such an overstatement we can all surely disprove from our own experience. Before my own conversion I knew only too disturbingly the drag and pull of depravity in my moral nature. According to the usual phrase, I called it my "lower nature". Yet just as certainly I was conscious of hereditary *good* urges and desires.

There was a "higher nature". I wanted somehow to know and to please God. I genuinely longed to be and do good. At times my longings and strivings after good were even painful. I had many thoughts and desires which I knew (and still know) were sincere and wholesome. What though someone objects that although I desired to be good I was not *actually* so? No objector can deny that the very *desire* after goodness is *good desire,* and is therefore an evidence of hereditary good in our moral nature.

Let us never forget that the Bible, along with its uncompromising exposure of human depravity, consistently documents the co-existence of innate good in man. The very Law given through Moses is an address to *that*, just as it is a warning against giving way to the evil. If it is not a challenge to something in man which can respond, it is a farce.

Not only in the Law, however, but up and down its pages the Bible recognises this presence of hereditary good. Joseph, about 1700 B.C., was not a born-again believer in our evangelical sense; but what a lovely character! He and his brothers are not presented as though one was regenerate and the other eleven were *un*regenerate. No, all twelve move before us just as they were by nature. Yet as their thoughts, words, doings, are narrated, do we not see an unmistakable intermingling of good and evil? Is not Joseph a beautiful character both by heredity and godly self-endeavour? Who will honestly deny the presence of goodness *there*, when even *God* speaks only commendation without one word of criticism? There are many such instances in both Old and New Testaments.

Who will deny that many a *mother's* love is the genuine goodness of a Christlike, self-sacrificing otherism, even though the mother may know little or nothing about the revelation of God in Christ? What about the statement in Acts 10: 35, spoken of an unconverted Italian military officer?—"In every nation he that feareth Him [God] and worketh righteousness is *accepted of Him.*" What about the statement in Romans 2: 7, which is written, not of Christian believers in particular, but of mankind in general?—"God . . . will render to every man according to his deeds: to them who by patient continuance in well doing seek for glory and honour and immortality, eternal life. . . . Tribulation and anguish upon every soul of man that doeth evil. . . . But glory, honour and peace to every man that worketh good. . . ."

Whatever problems those statements may conjure up in some minds as to the ultimate salvation of men, this at least will be conceded, that we are not here airing what we ourselves may *think*; we are quoting what the inspired Word itself says; and there is clear recognition of innate good as well as transmitted evil in human nature.

Furthermore, is not the predicted final, general judgment of our human race at the Great White Throne a climactic signature to this moral duality of our fallen nature? What is that final "judgment"? Is it an indiscriminate consignment of utterly and incorrigibly rotten human sinners to a damnation which was a foreknown inevitability because of their constitutional inability to obey one syllable of the Law which now dooms them? If it were any such assize as that, it would be a gigantic, theatrical monstrosity. On the contrary, however, it is to be an infallible judicial inquisition, and a resultant verdict based on the inborn sense of human accountability and the inherent struggle between the good and the evil in men. That judgment presupposes that the *good* is the rightful hereditary owner, and *evil* an hereditary intruder to be resisted.

Of course, no hereditary good in men can constitute a soul-saving *merit*, for the two reasons: (1) it does not obliterate the coexisting hereditary corruption, (2) it does not negate the legal *guilt* of sins committed. In other words, it still leaves man a sinner both by nature and behaviour.

Fallen man's condition may be defined in brief as: (a) spiritually dead, (b) morally diseased, (c) physically moribund. One important distinction which many Calvinists need to recognise is, that although man is *spiritually* dead and needs regeneration into new spiritual life, he is not *morally* dead, even though sadly perverted. He is not only *alive* to moral good, but is constitutionally bound to appreciate it when it is truly perceived, however much he may resist it. Being spiritually dead, man is utterly unable to regenerate himself; but being morally alive he *can* at least respond to the *truth* which regenerates. What theological battles have been waged on the question of human "ability" or "inability"!

Through failure (as just mentioned) to realize that although man is spiritually dead he is *not* also morally dead, a prominent Calvinist dogma has been that an unconverted man is utterly *unable* to perform any real moral good or even to respond to the

Gospel. He thus becomes helplessly passive. If he is one of the elect, he will be saved, whether he seeks it or not. If he is *not* one of the elect, he will *not* be saved, however much he may pray and long to be. Hence we get strange doctrines like that of so-called "limited atonement", i.e. limited to cover only the limited elect; and a teaching of predestination which is nothing but a religious fatalism. What confusion!—through making hereditary human depravity more deep and damning than the Bible actually teaches!

Most certainly man is morally alive, the evidences of which are all around us in the unabating struggle between hereditary good and hereditary evil. Going with this, just as certainly, men are free-willed either to accept or reject the Gospel. If that were not so, John 3: 16 and the divinely issued offer of a "whosoever will" salvation to "all men everywhere" would be a hollow mockery. Let me say it again for emphasis: fallen man absolutely cannot regenerate himself, but he *can* respond to the *truth* which regenerates.

I hold to the New Testament doctrine of election as firmly as anyone; but I believe that many Calvinists confuse divine fore-*knowing* with divine fore-*determining*. My outcry is against *any* doctrine of a limited "elect" which implies the fearful corollary that the God who bled as incarnate Love on Calvary *pre-destined* hundreds of millions of human beings, who could not help either being born or being born sinners, to a never-ending Gehenna. That simply *cannot* be true, for it contradicts forthright statements of Holy Writ. Here is one, from I Timothy 2: 4–6,

"GOD OUR SAVIOUR . . . WILL HAVE *ALL* MEN TO BE SAVED, AND TO COME TO THE KNOWLEDGE OF THE TRUTH.
"FOR THERE IS ONE GOD, AND ONE MEDIATOR BETWEEN GOD AND MEN, THE MAN CHRIST JESUS; WHO GAVE HIMSELF A RANSOM FOR *ALL*."

When I turn from such clear Scripture to the Westminster Confession I can only shudder to read in chapter 3,

"By the decrees of God, for the manifestation of His glory, some men and angels are predestinated unto everlasting life, and others *fore-ordained to everlasting death*."

"The rest of mankind [other than the elect] God was pleased . . . to *ordain* them to dishonour and *wrath* for their sin, to the praise of His glorious justice."

How such a ghastly, endless doom, forefixed before their birth upon helplessly handicapped humans, can be "glorious justice"(!) is beyond my own comprehension. I believe *all* that the Bible teaches on Hades, the "wrath to come", final judgment, and an ultimate Gehenna; but the sullen dogma of a predestined mass damnation is a God-dishonouring distortion, not real Biblical truth. I ask those of you whom I now address to reject it, and to reject also that exaggerated representation of hereditary *depravity* which is bound up with it.

I warn again that if we accept the Westminster categories on hereditary depravity, real *sanctification* of heart and life becomes a shimmering mirage which vanishes as we struggle toward it. Glance back to the sections already quoted, and see how inevitably they involve denial of experiential sanctification:

". . . *wholly* defiled in *all* the faculties and parts of soul and body."
". . . *utterly* indisposed, disabled, and *made opposite* to all good, and *wholly* inclined to *all* evil."
"This corruption of nature, during this life, doth remain in those that are regenerated . . . yet both itself and *all* the motions thereof are truly and properly *sin*."

Such dreary extremism with its "wholly", "utterly", "all", sin and badness, and a total "corruption" which must remain unchangeably within us Christians to our dying day, turns the New Testament promise of sanctification into a charnel house of dead hopes. Our "land of promise" in Christ becomes a bleak tundra. Any possibility of a transforming inward renewal of our nature disappears as completely as Atlantis beneath the ocean depths.

"If all this is true," laments A. M. Hills, "hard indeed is the lot of mankind. It is the fable of Sisyphus forever rolling the stone up the hill, the top of which it can never reach. We are the unfortunate Sisyphus. Our character is the stone. Holiness is the goal at the top of the mountain, which can never be reached by any possible striving, but which we are commanded to reach: and on our quivering, straining back, paralysed with 'inability', is laid the lash of moral obligation! We might all cry out with one breath, 'God pity us!' But no, God Himself is the hard master who drives us to attempt the impossible feat, and pitilessly swings the lash! There is nothing for us here but a life of hopeless sinning, and consequent agony of heart. . . . To ask or command men to be holy under such conditions would be as vain as it would be to urge them to pray while you solemnly assured them that no prayer ever was, or ever could be answered."

Yet those solemn Westminster protocols insisting on this total, irreversible, irreducibly life-long corruptness are the standard formula according to which the thinking of multitudes has been shaped among English-speaking peoples, not to mention further extensions.

Let it not be thought that I fail to appreciate the overall value of the Westminster Confession and Catechisms. They are classic and monumental. By many they have been unreasonably treated as compendiums of abstract theological dogma, whereas until recent days, especially in Scotland, they have proved themselves wonderfully practical handbooks of Christian duty which have stamped themselves with profound good upon individual and national character. Only about one third of the widely used *Shorter* Catechism states creed; the majority of its questions and answers concern duty. In the *Larger* Catechism, the catechesis on the Ten Commandments is indeed a weighty, thorough, heart-searching exposition of the moral law. Let me pay my full meed of eulogy. But the grim overstatements on hereditary depravity and the consequent understatements on experiential sanctification are big, bad blemishes.

To you whom I now address, my counsel is: Turn away from that venerably attired error; for error is no less error whether it comes to us in the rags of prodigals or the robes of divines. The result of either overstating or understating Scripture is always the same; it leads to self-contradiction and deprivation of blessing. As examples of this take just one more quotation from the Westminster Confession.

"When God converteth a sinner and translateth him into the state of grace, he freeth him from his natural bondage under sin, and, by His grace alone, enableth him freely to will and to do that which is spiritually good; yet so as [i.e. in suchwise] that by reason of his remaining corruption, he doth not perfectly nor only will that which is good, but doth also *will that which is evil.*

"The *will* of man is made perfectly and immutably free to good alone in the state of glory *only.*"—chapter ɪɪ: 4 and 5.

Surely that is as strangely contrary as it is unscriptural: God enables us to will "that which is good", yet in suchwise as to confirm us to *"will that which is evil"*. Read it carefully again: that is what the wording says, and makes it all the plainer by its final asseveration that in the future "state of glory *only*" is the bound will made fully "free" from willing what is evil! How opposite to this is *Paul's* cry in Romans 7!—"To *will* [i.e. to will the good] is present with me, but how to perform that which is good I find not." The context shows that the *will* was wholly *for* the good and against the evil. Then chapter 8 follows, showing that the will, "set free", is given also the power to *"do"* by the "Spirit of life in Christ Jesus". What about Hebrews 8: 10?—"I will put my laws into their minds, and write them in their hearts." In such renewed minds and hearts which *will* to do only God's will, can there be also a confirmed willing of "that which is evil"? Are there any limits to Philippians 2: 13?—"It is *God* who worketh in you, both to *will* and to *do* His good pleasure."

Christian believer, lay hold of it firmly and gratefully: you and I, as members of Christ, may be inwardly cleansed and *changed*. That is why Paul says, in 1 Timothy 1: 5, "The end of the commandment is love out of a *pure heart"*. That is why we read in Acts 15: 8, 9, of the Holy Spirit's *"purifying* their *hearts, through faith"*. That is why Ephesians 4: 23 tells us we may be "renewed" in the very *"spirit* of our *mind"*. This inwrought cleansing and renewal, this moral metamorphosis (Rom. 12:2) is one of the most precious and prominent reiterations of the New Testament epistles. Yes, we may be "transformed through the complete renewing of our minds" into full conformity to the "good and acceptable and perfect will of God"; and that indeed is *sanctification*.

SANCTIFICATION AND THE DIET LAW

"After submitting the Mosaic law to the most rigid test of modern scientific standards, the writer is convinced that Moses himself is a true modern—a radical scientist of the most advanced school. He is even seen to be leading most of our present-day scientists in the popular and important studies of bacteriology, psychology, physiology, hygiene, botanic chemistry, practical eugenics, sanitary sciences, quarantine principles, zoology, geology."

Thomas H. Nelson,
The Mosaic Law in the
Light of Modern Science.

SANCTIFICATION AND THE DIET LAW

WE MAY say with little hesitation that if only certain truths expressed in this chapter can be firmly planted in the minds of some whom we now address, years of poor health may be avoided, and years of buoyant vigour engendered.

That may sound rather like "tall talk" but it ,is true; and it has to do with the relationship of the New Testament saint to the Old Testament law. Millions of us are needing to learn today that the truest way to consistent health is the sanctification of the body in accordance with the physical health laws given to us from God Himself through Moses.

THE MOSAIC LAW AND OUR SALVATION

As a prelude to our comments on this, let us clarify our thinking as to what is the true relationship of the Christian to the Mosaic law. In these days when among the many new cults which have appeared, some are widely propagating the resurrected error that Christians must not only believe on our Lord Jesus, but also keep the moral law given through Moses, in order to be saved, there is new need to hoist aloft the vital New Testament truth that Christian believers are not under any such obligation to the Mosaic law. Unless one's thinking is out of kilter through wrong theory, the force and finality of statements like Romans 6: 14 are surely plain beyond any misunderstanding: *"YE ARE NOT UNDER THE LAW, BUT UNDER GRACE."*

That Epistle to the Romans is the Magna Charta of our Christian liberation from all bondage to the Mosaic law. On the one hand, "By the deeds of the law there shall no flesh be justified" (3: 20), but on the other hand, "Christ is the *end* of the law for *righteousness* to every one that believeth" (10: 4).

The epistle runs in three main movements. Chapters 1 to 8 are doctrinal, and their subject is, how the Gospel *saves the sinner*. Chapters 9 to 11 are dispensational, and their subject is, how the Gospel *relates to Israel*. Chapters 12 to 16 are mainly practical, and their subject is how the Gospel *relates to conduct*.

In part one (chapters 1–8) Paul first shows man's *need* for the Gospel. Both Jew and Gentile are (a) legally guilty—by continuous transgression, (b) morally depraved—by hereditary corruption. Then, from chapter 3: 21 onwards, he shows how the Gospel *meets* that need. The whole divine philosophy of salvation, as elucidated in those masterly eight chapters, is that we are saved in Christ by becoming (1) judicially *dead,* and (2) spiritually *alive.* More specifically—

> Judicially *dead*—dead to Sin and to the Law,
> Spiritually *alive*—by "the Spirit of life in Christ Jesus".

The *focus* is chapter 6: "Dead indeed unto sin, but alive unto God." The *climax* is chapter 8: "That the righteousness of the law might be fulfilled in us, who walk not after the flesh but after the Spirit." We cannot open this up here in detail,[1] but undoubtedly the gist of Paul's exposition is:

1. Legally *freed* in Christ from all bondage to the law as obligatory to soul salvation;
2. Spiritually *alive* in Christ and *fulfilling* the law in the truest spiritual sense.

The manifesto of our emancipation is finally crystallised in chapter 8: 1–4. Because I have become judicially dead in Christ (in whose all-including death I died and paid the penalty of the law) there is "therefore now no condemnation". All overhanging guilt is cleared away for ever, so that being thus freed legally I may also be freed *inwardly* by "the Spirit of life in Christ Jesus" whose renewing of my mind enables me spontaneously to fulfil the spiritual requirements of the divine law.

Yes, that is the resplendent liberation which is ours in Christ; and the capital truth which accompanies it is this, that we Christian believers are no longer struggling to keep the law in order to *be* saved, but by our new life in the Spirit we are spontaneously living out the precepts of the law because we *are* saved. That triumphant truth is written so boldly in the New Testament epistles that I, for one, am puzzled how anyone can miss it. The following are key verses and they should be unhurriedly pondered, for what they teach in clear statement is utterly vital to the true Gospel, and is being imperilled today in subtle new form.

---

[1] For fuller treatment see Romans in our work, *Explore the Book.*

"Justified by faith *apart from* the works of the law"—3: 28.

"Ye are *not under* the law, but under grace"—6: 14.

"Ye were made *dead* to the law through the body of Christ"—7: 4.

"We have been *discharged* from the law, so that we serve in newness of the spirit"—7: 6.

"Christ is the *end* of the law unto righteousness to every one that believeth"—10: 4.

"He that *loveth* his neighbour hath *fulfilled* the law"—13: 8.

"*Love* is the fulfilling of the law"—13: 10.

Could the pen of inspiration have written more perspicuously our absolute deliverance from all *debt* to the law?—from all *bondage* to the law?—and from all *obligation* to the law as a means to our salvation? Think of it: justified "*apart* from the law"; and "*not* under the law"; and "*dead* to the law"; and "*discharged* from the law". Yet our Seventh Day Adventists tell us that if we are to be saved we must keep the law *besides* trusting in Christ as our Saviour. Their contention is, that we must distinguish between the ceremonial law and the *moral* law, the latter being focally expressed in the Ten Commandments. That the ceremonial law is now done away in Christ they readily concede, but the Ten Commandments, so they argue, are the immutable divine standard of righteousness which can *never* be abrogated, and must therefore *ever* remain binding upon us.

Our first rebuttal of this is, that *nowhere* does the New Testament make such a distinction between the ceremonial law and the moral law in the various places where it declares our *freedom* from the law. As a matter of exactitude, if we are to partition the Mosaic law into its main components, it is not twofold ("ceremonial" and "moral") but threefold:

1. The "Commandments"—covering Israel's *moral* life (Ex. 19, 20).
2. The "Judgments"—covering Israel's *social* life (Exod. 21–23).
3. The "Ordinances"—covering Israel's *religious* life (Exod. 25 and onwards through Leviticus).

Now it should always be remembered that this threefold Mosaic law, with its detailed theocratic accompaniments, was never given to any nation outside Israel. There is no evidence anywhere to show that it was ever binding except exclusively within the covenant nation. But even if it *were* applicable outside Israel, no one can controvert this, that when the New Testament declares the law "done away" in Christ, it gives not the slightest fleck of a hint that any part is excepted or still binding.

Our High Calling

Does that negate or dishonour the Ten Commandments as a divine standard of righteousness? Not at all. One after another those commandments reappear up and down our New Testament epistles as parts of those Christian ethics which all the born again gratefully seek to fulfil in thought and word and deed. Yet although those commandments thus reappear separatedly in the New Testament, they nowhere appear *together* as a "moral law" which we still have to keep in order to be saved; nor do they ever re-appear in the sense of having to be obeyed as a *supplementary* contribution to our Saviour's finished work of atonement. Those Old Testament commandments are most nobly honoured when they are spontaneously lived out by freed and sanctified Christian believers, not as a supposed *means* of salvation, but as a sure and delightful *evidence* of it.

It is because our well-meaning new legalists view the keeping of the Ten Commandments as partly contributory to salvation that they never have the joyous *certainty* of eternal salvation here and now. After a delightful time of pleasant argument with a Seventh Day Adventist leader, years ago, I asked him: "If, then, the keeping of the moral Law is necessary as well as faith in the saviourhood of Christ, can you, as a Seventh Day Adventist, know for sure, here in this life, that you are eternally saved?" After a brief, thoughtful pause, he replied simply, "No". I then turned to John 3: 36, "He that believeth on the Son *HATH* everlasting life", and to 1 John 5: 13, "These things have I written unto you that believe on the Name of the Son of God, that ye may *know* that ye *HAVE* eternal life"—and to Romans 5: 1, 9; 8: 1, 38, 39.

Again, it is because Seventh Day Adventism preaches this concept of obligation to the Ten Commandments as the "moral law" that it rejects *Sunday* as the day to observe as a Christian "Sabbath", and insists that we must keep the *seventh*-day sabbath as enjoined in the fourth Commandment. But when the New Testament says that we are no longer under the law, not only does it completely ignore the Seventh Day Adventist distinction between the "moral" and the "ceremonial" law, it nowhere says that we must keep the seventh-day sabbath. On the contrary, from the resurrection of our Lord onwards, the New Testament puts all the emphasis on the *first* day of the week. That was the day on which our Lord arose. That was the day on which the Holy Spirit came at Pentecost to inaugurate the new dispensation of grace and of the *Ecclesia*. That was the day on which the earliest Christians met for their special fellowship and breaking of bread and contributing of gifts (Acts 20: 7; 1 Cor. 16: 2).

What is even more decisive, however, is the fact that while all other nine of the Ten Commandments reappear intermittently in the New Testament epistles, the fourth *nowhere* reappears. That which our Seventh Day Adventist friends make their most public issue is the very one which all those epistles leave out! The reason, of course, is obvious. Although the Ten Commandments collectively may rightly be called the "moral law" in epitome, yet to be strictly correct only nine of the ten are "moral"; the fourth commandment is *non*-moral; it is a purely non-moral injunction concerning a calendar *observance*.

Moreover, in Colossians 2: 14 the apostle Paul categorically asserts that the whole of the "moral law", i.e. the Ten Commandments, was put "out of the way", *including* the fourth commandment, so as never to hold us in the slightest bondage to it again. I quote direct from the Greek:

> "Having blotted out the against-us handwriting with the ordinances, which was contrary to us, and [He] took it out of the way, having nailed it to the Cross."

In that text the "handwriting" is the Greek *cheirographon*, a name for the Ten Commandments because they were the handwriting of God on the two tables of stone. Seventh Day Adventists tell us that it was the "ordinances" which were done away, *not* the "moral law". But they are wrong; for, as clearly as can be, Paul says that it was the "handwriting" (i.e. the Ten Commandments), not just the "ordinances", which was done away. Paul says that "*IT*" (not "they") was "nailed to the Cross". And *why* was "*IT*" blotted out? Because (says the text) it was "*against* us" and was "contrary to us". Yes, "*it*" was condemningly "against" us, but the "ordinances" *never* were, for they (the ordinances) pointed onwards to the One who should sacrifice Himself to save us.

No statement could be plainer: "it", the moral law, along with the whole Mosaic economy, was forever put away as no longer obligatory to the saving of the soul.

As for our supposedly having to keep the seventh-day sabbath, Paul definitely says, NO. See verse 16, where he tells us that neither the seventh-day sabbath nor any of the other Israelite sabbaths (six of them) is binding on us:

"Let no one therefore judge you in eating or in drinking, or in respect of a feast, or of a new moon, or of the *sabbaths*, which are [merely] a shadow of the things to come: the body [or fulfilling reality] is *CHRIST*."

We know the sincerity of our seventh-day sabbatarian, but he is answerable to the written Word of God, and to our Lord Himself who wrote so clearly our liberation from the Mosaic law—so clearly indeed that the obligation-to-the-law error is the less excusable. It is a strange wonder to me that any can be so dim-sighted to clear pronouncements like that of Galatians 3: 24, 25,

"The law was our schoolmaster—to Christ, that we might be justified by faith. But now that faith is come we are *no longer under* [*that*] *schoolmaster*."

How plain and how serious is the warning a bit later, in chapter 5: 4, "Ye who would be justified by the law are *fallen from grace*". It was not that the Judaistic teachers who subverted the Galatians were *denying* salvation through the Gospel; but they were *supplementing* it (supposedly) by doing that which our seventh-day legalists are now doing in their own way. What Apostolic authority, what jealous concern to preserve the Gospel from all such adulteration rings out in chapter 5! —

"STAND FAST THEREFORE IN THE LIBERTY WHEREWITH CHRIST HATH MADE US FREE, AND BE NOT ENTANGLED AGAIN WITH THE YOKE OF BONDAGE" (Gal. 5: 1).

Thank God, we Christian believers are eternally saved, here and now, by grace alone on God's part, through faith alone on ours, without any admixture of Moses with Christ, or of law with grace, or of works with faith, or of the flesh with the Spirit. Let us rejoice more than ever in our liberation from all bondage to the Mosaic law, and give all glory to the God of our salvation!

2. THE MOSAIC PHYSICAL REGULATIONS

But now, having reaffirmed our complete freedom in Christ from bondage to the law so far as the salvation of the *soul* is concerned, we would just as decidedly advocate obeying that law, in its physical enjoinments, with a view to the health of the *body*. Let every Christian clearly appreciate this fact, that although the Law is abrogated as a means of our eternal salvation, it has never been superseded as a God-appointed enjoinment for our temporal well-being. It is an unrepealed standard of moral and physical behaviour, the honouring of which always engenders health and prosperity, while the flouting of it always incurs inescapable ill-effects.

The Dietary Law

Included in the "judgments" or "statutes" of the Mosaic law there is what may be described as the *dietary code*. Whenever we read it we should always say to ourselves, "This is God speaking". If anyone knows what is proper for the body, He who made it does. I believe that many of our race's bodily ills would begin at once to disappear if we observed merely the main *proscriptions* of the Mosaic dietary guide.

Blood Forbidden

To begin with, there is the solemn injunction against imbibing animal *blood*.

"Moreover ye shall eat no manner of blood, whether it be of fowl or of beast, in any of your dwellings. Whatsoever soul it be that eateth any manner of blood, even that soul shall be cut off from his people" (Lev. 7: 26, 27).

"And whatsoever man there be of the house of Israel, or of the strangers that sojourn among you, that eateth any manner of blood; I will even set my face against that soul that eateth blood, and will cut him off from among his people. For the life of the flesh is in the blood: and I have given it to you upon the altar to make an atonement for your souls: for it is the blood that maketh an atonement for the soul. Therefore I said unto the children of Israel, No soul of you shall eat blood, neither shall any stranger that sojourneth among you eat blood. And whatsoever man there be of the children of Israel, or of the strangers that sojourn among you, which hunteth and catcheth any beast or fowl that may be eaten; he shall even pour out the blood thereof, and cover it with dust. For it is the life of all flesh; the blood of it is for the life thereof: therefore I said unto the children of Israel, Ye shall eat the blood of no manner of flesh: for the life of all flesh is the blood thereof: whosoever eateth it shall be cut off" (Lev. 17: 10–14).

"Only be sure that thou eat not the blood: for the blood is the life; and thou mayest not eat the life with the flesh. Thou shalt not eat it; thou shalt pour it upon the earth as water. Thou shalt not eat it; that it may go well with thee, and with thy children after thee, when thou shalt do that which is right in the sight of the Lord" (Deut. 12: 23–25).

So, not only were some animals forbidden, as being in themselves unclean, but the blood even of the "clean" animals was thus emphatically excluded from diet. Notice: the reason for this was, "that it may go well with thee and thy children". God did not give those "laws" to Israel merely for the sake of testing their obedience to peculiar requirements. No, those requirements were for their moral and mental and physical well-being. Underlying them all is Deuteronomy 5: 29, "That it might be *well with them* and with their children for ever".

With large measure of truth it has been often said in recent years, by outstanding medical men, "You are what you eat". That may not seem so seriously true at a cursory glance, but it proves to be true enough in due course; for in these days not only have we discovered as never before how greatly the mind affects the body, but we are now learning more clearly how the *body reacts* upon the *mind*. Many who have committed suicide, or who have succumbed to psychopathic ailments, would never have done so if their bodily condition had been different.

Dr. Adelle Davis, in *Let's Eat Right to Keep Fit*, says, "In one of the mental hospitals in the South, every incoming patient must eat a completely adequate diet for two months before being put into a general ward. During this time a large per cent of the patients recover completely and are sent home" (p. 93).

I read quite recently about a woman who became addicted to strange outbursts of violent temper, until a danger-point was reached at which she had to be put into a mental hospital. Her trouble seemed not only inexplicable, but hopeless, until a certain doctor who had known her well for years asked if he might be allowed to treat her at his own risk. He knew her prevailing diet, her continual resort to certain drugs, and of an intestine disorder which had latterly become acutely aggravated. He suspected a cause-and-effect relation between the physiological and the psychological, and he proved right; for under his care, which mainly consisted of seeing that she had a scientifically nutritious diet, she became completely cured and permanently normal again.

Dr. Paul Dudley White, President Eisenhower's doctor, has written, "I would emphasize soundness of body, mind and spirit

—all three. Too long have we allowed ourselves to be dominated by psychosomatic or 'mind over matter' philosophy, with little concern for somatopsychic, or 'body over spirit' physiology. Yet there is no doubt that good physical health affects the spirit as much as a good spirit affects health."

The late Louis Kuhne, a German medical specialist, conducted all his curative work on the basic axiom that "the beginning of all disease is in the blood". I believe that his dictum is axiomatic of the lower animals as well as of man. If an animal has a disease, that disease either comes *from* a blood condition or else it *registers* first in the blood, since the blood continually courses through the whole organism. It is possible for one physical organ to be diseased without the other organs of the body being affected for a time; but the blood is affected at once. Also, whatever may be in the stomach, good or bad, food or poison, the blood gets it and distributes it throughout the anatomy.

Furthermore, dead blood, i.e. blood in deceased bodies, is most susceptible to putrefaction and decay. Not without reason do we marvel at the skill of ancient embalmers. Bodies of Egyptian royalties have been preserved thousands of years. But not all the clever embalmers in ancient Egypt could have halted putrefaction and decomposition without at once first draining away the blood from the corpse. It is my opinion that our modern abattoir leaves too much blood in the flesh of herd animals; and with poultry there is strangling rather than blood-draining. It is greatly noteworthy that at the First ecumenical council in Church history (Acts 15: 1–35) all Gentile believers were set completely free from obligation to keep the Law of Moses so long as they abstained from imbibing blood, along with one or two other practices considered impure. In reply to the Pharisaic sect who would have had Gentile believers "keep the law of Moses", Peter expostulated, "Why tempt ye God to put a yoke upon the neck of the disciples which neither our fathers nor we were able to bear?" (10). The upshot of the deliberation was this resolution:

"Forasmuch as we have heard that certain . . . have troubled you . . . saying ye must keep the Law. . . . It seemed good unto us, being assembled with one accord, to send chosen men unto you with our beloved Barnabas and Paul . . . who shall also tell you the same things by mouth. For it seemed good to the Holy Spirit, and to us, to lay upon you no greater burden than these necessary things: That ye abstain from meats offered to idols, and from *blood*, and from things *strangled*, and from fornication; from which if ye keep yourselves, ye shall do well" (24–29).

Let Seventh Day Adventists and certain others note this well: If there is one place where the seventh-day sabbath would have been enjoined if our observance of it had been necessary, it is here, in this formal Apostolic ruling under the dictate of the Holy Spirit: but there is not a mention. Let all the rest of us ponder the solemn reiteration of the Mosaic health code against imbibing *blood* with animal flesh. The prohibition of blood is *not* a "must" for soul-salvation, but it is a "must" for physical cleanness with a view to maximal health.

There are those who may make light of it; but those who will be wiser than God usually pay dearly. Especially in these days when, through the enormous use of chemical fertilizers and poison sprays, diseases in plants and cattle have increased, the divine interdict against the imbibing of blood is all the more well worth regarding.

Animal Fat Forbidden

Another very definite ruling of the Mosaic dietary manual is against human consumption of animal *fat*:

"Ye shall eat *no manner of fat*, of ox, or of sheep, or of goat. And the fat of the beast that dieth of itself, and the fat of that which is torn with beasts, may be used in any other use: but ye shall in no wise eat of it" (Lev. 7: 23, 24).
"It shall be a perpetual statute for your generations throughout all your dwellings, that ye *eat neither fat* nor blood" (3: 17).

All around us today we are seeing the tell-tale penalties of ignoring this divine statute. Heart disease has now become number one killer in U.S.A., Canada, Britain, Europe, Australia, New Zealand; and scientists are increasingly persuaded that *fat* is the traitor betraying us to the assassin. Too much fat in *food* eventually means too much fat in the *blood*, then too much fat in the *arteries* in the form of cholesterol, then too much cholesterol in the coronaries, resulting in coronory thrombosis and "heart attack". Admittedly, an over-cholesterol condition can be due to genetic and other factors, but the greatest single cause is animal fat in the diet. Also, much that goes by the name of heart disease is not strictly disease of the heart itself, but atherosclerosis, i.e. the accumulation of cholesterol in the coronaries to the point where blood-clot or cholesterol blockage prevents the blood from getting *into* the heart.

There are aspects of heart disease and coronary lesions on which medical opinion is divided, but most now agree that atherosclerosis is due to faulty fat metabolism caused by over-fat in the diet. Experiments have confirmed this beyond all peradventure. Arteriosclerosis has been quickly produced in test animals purely by diet high in fat but poor in protein. During the past fifty years or more, Americans and Europeans have been increasingly substituting fats for carbohydrates. We are using more and more butter, fried fish, fried chicken, and fried potatoes, fritters, doughnuts, etc., and more fat with meat than ever. Now the fact is, that Nature supplies *all* the fat we humans need in foods *apart* from animal flesh. In other words, so long as we have an all-round diet, we do not need, nor should we ingest, the fat of animals. When we persist in doing so, we invite trouble.

A parallel may be made between this and diabetes. All the sugar our bodies require is obtainable in the various foods and fruits which Nature provides. On entering the body this sugar is transmuted into glucose which provides us with energy; but the body cells are unable to utilize glucose normally without insulin supplied by the pancreas. When, in addition to the sugar which natural foods supply, we keep adding cane-sugar, in tea, coffee, puddings, ice-cream, syrups, candies, colas, "cokes", "pops" and "ades", a point often comes at which the exhausted pancreas flunks and says, "I give up!" The unusable sugar spills over into the blood and the urine—and there is diabetes. A specialist in internal medicine told me not long since that one out of every *four* people in U.S.A. today gets diabetes in latent, incipient, chronic or severer form! Yes, and I also read in an article on heart disease as the "Number One Killer", that one out of every *three* Americans today can "expect to die from a damaged heart".

How much wiser we would be to observe the dietary counsels of the divine Law given through Moses rather than the palate-tickling advertisements of many modern food firms! This forbidding of animal fat is for our good. As we often bring on diabetes by continually adding refined *sugar itself* to Nature's normal provision, so do we make ourselves liable to heart trouble,

strokes, and high blood pressure through the continual consuming of animal *fat itself* in addition to the fat and oils which
Nature normally supplies in an adequate diet. Nor is even that
all: as I now write these lines I chance to notice that Dr. A. E.
Blackburn (who conducted *cancer* research all over the world)
says in his book on the subject, that he found an *absence* of
gastric cancer in countries "where *animal fat* is not part of the
food". The famous Dr. Bircher Benner of Zurich, also, avers
that "excess of *fats*, sugars and starches are causes of *all* nutritional disease".

Unclean Animals

Outright vegetarianism is not taught in the Bible. In the diet
divinely specified for man in his original condition (Gen. 1: 29;
2: 9, 16) flesh was not included. After the Fall, when physiological changes had been hereditarily transmitted and distributed,
flesh *was* included (Gen. 9: 2–4). Later, in the authentic divine
diet-code of the Mosaic economy, animal flesh is again permitted,
but at the same time restricted. Certain animals are categorised
as "unclean", and their flesh is strictly prohibited, as being un-
suitable for human consumption. Take Leviticus 11: 7, 8:

"And the swine, though he divide the hoof, and be clovenfooted,
yet he cheweth not the cud; he is unclean to you. Of their flesh *shall
ye not eat*, and their carcase shall ye not touch; they are unclean to
you."

A repeat of this occurs in Deuteronomy 14: 3, 8, and a significant echo in Isaiah 65: 2–4.

"I have spread out my hands all the day unto a rebellious people,
which walketh in a way not good, after their own thoughts; a people
that provoketh Me to anger continually to My face; that sacrificeth
in gardens, and burneth incense upon altars of brick . . . *which eat
swine's flesh, and broth of abominable things* in their vessels."

Why should the hog be prohibited? In Leviticus 11: 1–8, the
animals permitted for human food are: "Whatsoever parteth
the hoof, and is clovenfooted, and cheweth the cud." The hog is
excepted because, "though he divide the hoof, and is clovenfooted, yet *he cheweth not the cud*". Let me quote Elmer A.
Josephson in *God's Key to Health and Happiness*.

"The clean animals that chew the cud and have a divided hoof such as the ox, sheep, goat, deer, cow, steer, buffalo, etc., because of the sacculated condition of the alimentary canal and the secondary cud receptacle, have practically three stomachs as refining agencies and cleansing laboratories, for the purifying of their food. This cleanses their systems of all poisonous and deleterious matter. It takes their clean vegetable food over *twenty-four hours* to be be turned into flesh, which flesh even the pre-Mosaic law said was clean. This was not mere 'ceremonial' cleansing, but it was made hygienically and physiologically clean and wholesome (pp. 32, 33).

"In comparison, we find that the swine's (hog) anatomy, as a supplement to his bad appetite (eating any putrid thing he finds), has but one poorly constructed stomach arrangement, and very limited excretory organs generally. Consequently, in about *four hours* after he has eaten his polluted swill and other putrid and offensive matter, man may eat the same, second-handed off the ribs of the pig."

But maybe someone will be asking why God *made* "unclean" animals. There is a clear answer, and again we cannot do better than quote Mr. Josephson:

"Some ask, 'Why did the Lord make the unclean animals?' They were created as scavengers; as a rule they are meat-eating animals that clean up anything that is left dead in the fields, etc. If a dog (or any animal whatsoever) should die in the field and lie in the sun and bloat, until it is broken open and the maggots and putrefaction set in, then the swine or other scavengers will come and eat up all this filth and putrid matter, hereby keeping disease germs from spreading over the earth and killing off mankind. Scavengers were never created for human consumption.

"The God-given Mosaic law condemns this meat, manufactured out of the filthiest and most abominable matter, as *unclean*. In its very nature it is poisonous, diseased and deadly. The flesh of the swine is said by many authorities to be the prime cause of much of our American ill health, causing blood diseases, weakness of the stomach, liver troubles, consumption, cancers, tumours, eczema, etc." (p. 33).

Many pages might be written giving instances of the baneful results from eating swine's flesh. I am fully aware that many a doctor may not credit this, but I would respectfully add that some of the most outstanding medical men whom I have met are alive to it. Is it altogether without significance that today "Israel has the lowest death rate in the world" (the very words of Prime Minister David Ben Gurion in 1962)? Is it not because the Israeli State is observing the Mosaic dietary code? The Israeli parliament by an overwhelming vote has banned the "raising, keeping or slaughtering" of pigs (except in a few centres which have a large "Christian" population).

One of the diseases most to be dreaded is *trichinosis*, caused by the trichina worm. The deadly trichina worm seems especially generated and distributed by the flesh of the hog. This sinister parasite often exists in myriads in pork, often so minute as to elude even the microscope. Mr. Elmer Josephson quotes from Laird S. Goldsborough in a past issue of *Reader's Digest,* "A single serving of infected pork—even a single mouthful—can kill or cripple or condemn the victim to a lifetime of aches and pains". So far as I know there is still no cure, no drug or other specific to defeat this dread disease. Mr. Josephson quotes Senator Thomas C. Desmond, chairman of a New York Trichinosis Commission: "Physicians have confused trichinosis with some fifty ailments, ranging from typhoid fever to acute alcoholism." "That pain in your arm or leg may be arthritis or rheumatism; but it may be trichinosis. That pain in your back may mean a gall-bladder involvement; but it may mean trichinosis." I will add no more except that I incline to think, from things heard and read, that far more troubles come from eating pig (a "mobile garbage-disposal unit") than many suspect.

Now of course the various parts of the hog can be made so savoury, and the rearing of pigs is so financially profitable, and so many of us are too prejudiced to be advised, that the red lamp of divine warning may be disregarded; but I say again that those who will be wiser than God invite sore troubles. Let every Christian ponder well the words of 2 Corinthians 6: 17 to 7: 1 (it is a pity that the first verse of chapter 7 was not left as the last verse of chapter 6, which in reality it *is*).

"Wherefore come out from among them, and be ye separate, saith he Lord, and *TOUCH NOT THE UNCLEAN*; and I will receive you, ınd will be a Father unto you, and ye shall be my sons and daughters, aith the Lord Almighty. Having therefore these promises, dearly beoved, let us cleanse ourselves from all *FILTHINESS OF THE FLESH* and spirit, completing holiness in the fear of God."

I think it is pretty certain that when Paul speaks about this cleansing of ourselves from all "filthiness of the *flesh*" he is including the forbidden eating of swine's flesh.

So stubbornly do some resent the injunction to abstain from swine's flesh, they try to argue that Peter's vision in Acts 10 removes the ban on it. But they are wrong. Glance back at the vision. Peter sees a sheet let down from heaven, containing "all manner" of animals and fowl. There comes a voice, "Rise, Peter, kill, and eat," to which Peter replies, "Not so, Lord, for I have never eaten anything that is common or unclean". Then the voice says, "What God hath cleansed call not thou common." Now to argue that God let that sheet down from heaven to tell Peter that certain unclean animals were now allowable for food is absurd. Peter himself certainly knew that it had no such meaning. Very quickly he grasped that the vision was symbolic of *persons*: "Of a truth," he exclaims, "I perceive that God is no respector of *persons*: but in every nation he that feareth Him, and worketh righteousness, is accepted with Him" (34, 35). As for the words, "What God hath *cleansed*", Peter himself tells us to what they referred. See Acts 15: 7–9, "Men and brethren, ye know how God made choice among us, that the *Gentiles* by my mouth should hear the word of the Gospel, and believe. And God, who knoweth the hearts, bare them witness, giving *them* the Holy Spirit, even as He did unto us: and put no difference between them and us, *CLEANSING* their hearts by faith."

To argue from Acts 10 that the Gospel now makes unclean beasts and birds and creeping things clean, or that the regeneration of our *souls* alters the digestive organs of our *bodies,* or that the glad tidings of salvation by grace annul the divine diet-code of good health through clean eating, is to grab at the wind.

No Finless Sea-foods

In a short article like this we can merely touch on matters which well deserve ample consideration. I would call attention to the divine disallowing of finless sea-beings for human food.

"And all that have not fins and scales in the seas and in the rivers, of all that move in the waters, and of any living thing which is in the waters, they shall be an abomination unto you. . . . Ye shall not eat of their flesh, but ye shall have their carcases in abomination" (Lev. 11: 10, 11).

Following this, there are prohibitions of certain fowl and of creeping things. One thing which strikes our attention is that the forbidden creatures are mainly, if not wholly, those which themselves live on an unclean or flesh diet. But there are other reasons, too, why the all-knowing divine Dietician forbade them to us. In these days there is a silly craze, especially in many "high class" public eating places, for savoury delicacies of all sorts—frogs, snails, oysters, and other even stranger items, the very thought of which nauseates some of us. Let those keep devouring divinely forbidden creatures who will; but are many of our strangest diseases unsuspectedly tied up therewith? Let those be wiser than God who choose. The laws of God operate everywhere throughout the universe. They must be obeyed or they automatically exact penalty. The greater the violation, the greater is the penalty, whether in the realm of physics, chemistry, hygiene, diet or morals. Being spiritually minded does not exempt us from the need to observe the rules of physical wellbeing. It is no use my praying for *healing* from sickness while by breaking health laws I am *causing* such sickness. Divine love may forgive us, but Nature *never* does.

We may sum up by saying that the Scripture diet emphasis is upon cereals, vegetables, fruits. Meat is included, but with such restrictions concerning blood and fat, unclean animals, birds, and forbidden aquatic creatures, as to indicate care and restraint in its use. Today, alas, in our intricately commercial world, our most important cereal, wheat, is being largely devitalized before it gets to the consumer. In each whole grain of wheat, largely in the bran coatings, there is phosphorous, lime, magnesium, chlorine, carbon, iron, sodium, silicon, potassium, sulphur, manganese, nitrogen, iodine, oxygen, hydrogen, while the wheat *germ* is rich in choline and natural oils. But the general thing in these days, for commercial reasons (packing, dispatching, preserving, etc.) is to remove the wheat germ, bleach the remainder with chemical (often harmful) and add some such preservative as calcium propionate. Such white bread, fed to test animals, has had grievous effects. White flour is devitalized, and is harmful to our human organism. At the very least, our tampering with wheat as Nature gives it steals from our most vital cereal much of its value.

Both white flour and white sugar are robbed of choline, an ingredient which acts as a corrective against cholesterol accumulation in veins and arteries—which latter is the prime cause of much that goes by the name of "heart failure". It has been truly observed: "Our sugar companies take this good natural food through fourteen steps of refinery. In this process we extract the B-complex, the enzymes, proteins, minerals and vitamins. We feed this precious 'by-product' of blackstrap molasses to our cattle. We people eat the lifeless remains, white sugar. Result:

strong cattle and weak people; healthy animals and crippled humans. . . . White sugar is dead. It can be stored in 100 pound sacks for years in filthy warehouses and still be sold for a good profit. The worms will not eat it. It holds nothing for them."

How important is proper diet! How many thousands today are in our over-crowded hospitals who never would have been there but for wrong eating! How many have inadvertently committed slow suicide with their knives and forks! Many of us have so perverted and enslaved our palates by devitalized taste-tickling dainties and savouries, that to eat food just as Nature supplies it now seems abnormal! With my Bible open before me I would say to all: keep off meat with the blood still in it. Keep off animal fats. Keep off all parts of the hog. Keep off all those forbidden land creatures and finless aquatic creatures which the Mosaic law disallows. Keep away as much as possible from white bread, white sugar, white rice. Look carefully at the wrapped, packaged or canned food-stuffs which you buy at the grocery stores. Keep away from all those sugary breakfast cereals which tell you the vitamins or minerals which the manufacturer has injected, but do *not* tell you all the vital elements which have been eliminated. Even if it costs more, get guaranteed whole-wheat bread; and as a cereal get pure wheat germ. Let the milk which you buy be that which is least artificially treated. Guard against buying those eating commodities which are marked as containing chemical preservatives, also those which have artificial flavourings and colourings.

I know the problem of keeping rigidly to this in these days; but do it as far as is possible, remembering always that one of the indispensable ways of keeping healthy is to eat *live* foods, fresh and untampered with, as Nature gave them. To offset the more or less devitalized foods which you perhaps cannot *altogether* avoid at the modern grocer's, eat regularly plenty of fresh vegetables, fruits, grains and nuts. I am not a vegetarian, but I acknowledge only too willingly that even when there is little or no flesh-meat in one's diet, that lack is negligible if sufficient nuts and grains are included. Indeed, such is the protein value of the soybean and certain others as to make flesh meat practically unnecessary. *Un*processed cheeses, and especially *cottage* cheese, are wonderfully rich, also, in proteins.

How many a life of gifted and powerful ministry has been cut short by inattention to these things! Christian sanctification let us never forget, has undoubted reference to the *body*. Let every Christian see to it that the *body* is given proper food, and sufficient *exercise* such as suits our years, and sufficient rest in *sleep*. Many who are now far from well in body, and therefore often depressed in mind, would cure themselves and enjoy restoration to untroubled slumber far sooner than they think, if only they would resolutely observe the foregoing safeguards, all of which have Scriptural authentification.

However, I will add no more, lest I should wander out of my own special province into that of the nutritionist or other physiological specialist. I cannot do better than conclude by saying: Observe the God-given dietary code of the Mosaic Law; eat *good* food; keep active; rest regularly; do not develop into a food fad or a diet crank; but so far as the problem of *modern* meat and grocery is concerned, think realistically, warily, and teachably. For wise and practical guidance in this area you could much profit by reading carefully, two or three times, Dr. Adelle Davis's widely circulated book, *Let's Eat Right to Keep Fit*, or Dr. Catharyn Elwood's book, *Feel Like A Million*, which, I notice, is now issued in a cheap paperback edition. I am sure that such care, under such guidance, can spare us many ailments, lesser or worse, and engender years of continuing health, vigour, buoyancy, usefulness.

SANCTIFICATION AND THE CROSS

To Thee, dear Holy Spirit,
  I bring my worship now,
With reverent adoration
  In prayer to Thee I bow:
As truly as I worship
  The Father and the Son,
I worship Thee, blest Spirit,
  For Thou with Them art one.

The truth of my salvation
  By Thee alone I know;
My union with the Saviour
  To Thee alone I owe:
My long-unseen Redeemer
  Would now be lost to me
Were not His now-indwelling
  Made real within by Thee.

By Thee *alone*, blest Spirit,
  My Saviour works within
To purify and change me,
  And break the hold of sin:
His cross, His resurrection,
  Would powerless wonders be
Unless thro' Thee, dear Spirit,
  He lived and wrought in me.

                    J.S.B.

SANCTIFICATION AND THE CROSS

IN THE conventional form of holiness teaching today there is a certain peculiar feature which seems so Scriptural and so widely endorsed that apparently few Christians ever think of questioning it. Indeed, it has become so acceptedly central to the usual system of sanctification doctrine that one might well call it the sensitive nerve-centre. Yet according to strict exegesis (so I maintain) it is demonstrably unsound and should be rejected.

To thousands of believers it has seemed at first like the truly Scriptural, heaven-planned way of deliverance from "inbred sin" or the so-called "old nature", but afterward it has proved factitious, leaving many a heart dazed with disappointment at the seeming untruthfulness of Scripture. My earnest concern in this present study is to exhibit its fallaciousness so as to guide the feet of at least some heavenward pilgrims away from it.

The teaching to which I refer is, that sanctification comes through an inward crucifixion of the believer with Christ; a subjectively experienced dying with Him on the Cross, and a "reckoning" oneself to be "dead indeed" unto sin from then onwards. More specifically, there are theoretically "two natures" in the born again, and sanctification comes through the crucifixion of the "*old* nature", or, according to usual phrase, "through our *identification* with Christ in His death, burial and resurrection".

I will not linger here on the similarity of this to some of the long-ago "mystery" cults, or to mediaeval and other forms of introversive mysticism. My three big concerns are: (1) it is being widely taught today, (2) it is not truly Scriptural, (3) it does much harm to many.

THE CURRENT TEACHING

As most of us are aware, it is the current teaching of well-known gatherings for the deepening of the spiritual life, and of characteristic literature on the subject. The following quotations, all from outstanding spokesmen, will give the doctrine in their own words. They are all accurately reported or transcribed, but although it is usual and proper to name the persons whom one quotes, I purposely leave these anonymous out of esteem for men whom I "love in the Lord", and whose teaching as a whole is grandly Scriptural.

1. "There, as we look upon that Cross, we see ourselves in Him; for He took this fallen nature of ours, this sin-principle within us, and put it to death on the Cross." "Tonight our Saviour is here, and He is telling us that He not only died *for* us, but also that we might die *with* Him . . . that the power of self in each one of us might be put out of action or destroyed."

2. "When Christ was crucified He took with Him to the Cross not only your sins but your sinful nature too. In some wonderful way, deeply mysterious but nevertheless true, your sinful *nature* was put to death on the Cross with Christ. . . . 'Our old man' writes Paul, 'is crucified with Him' (Rom. 6: 6). And he goes on, 'Reckon ye also yourselves to be dead indeed unto sin' (6: 11). As you reckon on this amazing fact, the power of it begins to be experienced in your life . . . your old nature is kept in the place of death, and its former power to make you sin has gone."

3. "Our old man, that is, our self-life, has been nailed to the Cross. Through our union with our Lord in His death we, in the purpose of God, have died to sin even as He died to it. We were one with Him in His grave and we are one with Him in His resurrection. That is our position objectively; but by *faith* we must make it *subjectively* real."

4. "When Christ died on the Cross to sin, we were *identified* with Him. . . . But it is not enough to know that historically all believers died with Christ; we must appropriate that truth if it is to be real in our experience. God reckons us dead to sin because of our union with Christ in *His* death to sin. Now, by faith, we must enter into God's reckoning. . . . God declares to all who cry out for deliverance from the tyranny of self that this self was crucified with Christ."

Now when a doctrine is not accurately Scriptural it inevitably slips into self-contradictions. That is conspicuously so in this instance. The identification theory is based on several statements in the Pauline epistles, mainly on Romans 6: 6, 11, and Galatians 2: 20. We shall show how incautiously those passages are misinterpreted; but first let us note the strange self-contradictions which accompany the four quotations just submitted. Not only are those four quotations sufficiently representative of the theory, but the naïve self-refutations affixed to them typically expose the inherent *inconsistency* of the theory.

Glance back at quotation number one. How definite it is that "this fallen nature of ours, this sin-principle within us" was indeed "put to death on the Cross" so that now "the power of self in each one of us might be put out of action"—yes, even "*destroyed*"! Yet close on the heels of that the preacher warns us: "We must never forget that in every one of us there is a fallen nature which we must carry *right through life*. We do not preach or teach in this place sinless perfection". So, after all, our "fallen nature" with its inherent "sin-principle" was *not* actually "put to death" on the Cross, neither is it "put out of action", much less "destroyed", inside the believer: it must be carried "right through life" to our last day on earth! And the preacher lamely explains: "We do not preach or teach in this place sinless perfection"—which is a mere cover-up (a very skimpy one) of his sudden retreat from the logical implication of his death-by-identification theory.

Look back now at the second of our four quotations. On the basis of Romans 6: 6 and 11 it assures me that my "sinful nature" or "old man" was crucified with Christ, and that therefore I may now "reckon" myself "dead indeed unto sin". It then adds, "As you reckon on this amazing fact, the power of it begins to be experienced in your life . . . your old nature is kept in the place of *death*". Yet now (how strangely!) the able author proceeds: "The understanding of this truth, that your 'old man' was 'crucified with Him', will help you when that old nature comes *clamouring for recognition* and seems likely to *entice you to sin*". So my so-called "old nature" is not dead at all, despite all my "reckoning"! On the contrary, it is just as much alive as ever, and "entices" me to sin! Yet even stranger is the author's further advice, "When the old nature rises up (as it will) with its promptings to sin . . . take your stand upon God's unshakeable fact, 'My old nature was done with for ever at the Cross'." So you are to keep on believing that it *was* done away on the Cross, and that it *is* done away from your heart, while all the time it is "clamouring" and "enticing" to sin within you! How blind to absurdity can obsession with a hyper-spiritual theory make us!

Take the third of our quotations. Its author is no longer on earth, but while he was here how I loved and admired him for his Christlike character and gifted ministry of the Word! He takes the usual view that the "old man" of Romans 6: 6 is our so-called old nature, or, as he here calls it, our "self-life" (a much-used but ambiguous phrase). That "self-life" was "nailed to the Cross", so he says, because we were "one with" our Lord "in His grave" and we are "one with Him in His resurrection".

So, then, says our author, "That is our position objectively; but by *faith* we must make it *subjectively* real". (This idea, that what happened *objectively* on the Cross has an intended counterpart *subjectively* in the believer is the very core of the identification theory. It is without Scriptural foundation, but we waive criticism for the moment). How then does this "objective" death of the "self-life" on Calvary *become* "subjectively real" in our experience? Queerly enough, our author now swings right round and says that the "self-life" (whatever part of us that means) has *not* died, but that "*we* (whatever remainder of us *that* means) are to die to *it.*" Here are his words: "We must regard ourselves as dead to sin and self . . . the self-life may not be dead, but *we* are to die to *it.*" So I am to regard *myself* ("we") as dead to my "*self*". Yet I am not *really* dead to my "self", I shall have to "*die* to it"! My "self-life" supposedly died "objectively", but it will *not* die "subjectively"; yet I am to make the objective subjective! Where are we?

Finally, look back at that fourth quotation. It flows from the pen of an expert, but it carries the same sort of contrariety. Ostensibly it brings just the message of liberation which many a heart in bondage is aching to hear. It tells us that through our being "identified" with Christ "God reckons us dead to sin", so that now, by "faith", *we* may "enter into God's reckoning". In fact (says the quotation) "God declares to all who cry out for deliverance from the tyranny of self that this self was crucified with Christ". Is not that a soul-thrilling proclamation of freedom? Well, the very pen which writes it now dashes our hopes to the ground by adding: "That freedom is only *potential*. It must be progressively realized in daily experience. . . . Not even the Christian will ever be free from *the drive to sin.*"

Judicial versus Experiential

So, then, our four representative quotations tell us successively that "this fallen nature of ours", or this "sin-principle", or our so-called "old nature", or our "self-life", or the "self", was "put to death", was "crucified", was "nailed to the Cross", in order that it might be "put out of action", or "kept in the place of death", and its power "destroyed" *within the believer*. Yet our four authors nevertheless warn us that the evil thing remains in us "right through life", and that it "clamours for recognition" and "entices to sin", and is "*not* dead", but *we* are somehow *yet* to "die to *it*"; and even then no Christian will "ever be free from the *drive* to sin"! If that is not, in John Bunyan's phrase, a "Mr. Looking-Both-Ways", I am strangely mistaken. Surely the palpable self-contradictoriness of it should so emphasize its invalidity as to put it out of court at once. Yet it persists on and on, due to a wrong concept of the believer's "identification" with the crucifixion of Christ.

I believe that this theory of death to sin by an inward crucifixion with Christ is error. I maintain, after unbiased study, that according to careful exegesis of the New Testament, the Christian believer's identification with the death of our Lord is *judicial*, not experiential; that it was *once-for-all*, and is not continually re-enactable; that it was *objective*, but not transferably subjective; that it was a judicial death *completed*, and is not a crucifixion still to be effected inside the believer; that it was a death to Sin and the Law in a *penal* and *legal* sense, not a death to some sinful "self" or inherited depravity in our nature; that it was a death *then* and *there*, and is not a protracted dying here and now. Yet however fully we may prove this, and however often we may say it, so thoroughly wedded are many Christians to the usual form of holiness teaching, they still persist in thinking that *somehow* the believer's long-ago *judicial* identification with the Cross must also become a *duplicated* identification in the believer's present-day experience. But the onus is on all who so argue to show us where it is taught in the New Testament: and they cannot do so, for the New Testament nowhere teaches it.

It is no use turning to Romans 6: 6, "Our old man is crucified with Him. . . ." Nay, in the Greek the verb is in the aorist: "Our old man *was* crucified with Him" (i.e. then and there, not "is" or "will be" here and now). Nor does that Paulinism, "our old man", refer to the believer's inner nature. If Paul had meant "nature" he would have used the proper Greek word, *phusis*, as he does elsewhere when he means· nature. In Romans 6: 6 the word is *anthropos*, "man", and the expression, "our old man" simply continues what Paul has been saying from chapter 5: 12

onwards about the old man (*anthropos*) Adam, through whom comes condemnation, and the new "man" (*anthropos*) Christ, through whom comes justification. "Our old man" is a Paulinism for the whole Adam *race* which, so Paul is telling us, was *judicially* sentenced and done away in the death of Christ— just as he again states in 2 Corinthians 5: 14, "If One died for all, then *all* died", i.e. in Him.

Nor is it any use turning to Romans 6: 11, "Likewise reckon ye also yourselves to be dead indeed unto sin", as though Paul were giving us warrant to reckon ourselves *inwardly* dead to hereditary sin-bias. Nay, that word, "likewise", means in the same way as (in the preceding verse) our Lord died unto sin "once for all" (Greek *ephapax*); but who among believers would dare to claim, "I have experienced that kind of once-for-all crucifixion, and it has brought an absolute inward death of my evil nature to sin"? Or who would claim to have experienced any such outright, permanent death of the "self" to the suppositionary "old nature" (if there is some subtle difference between the two!)? What Paul really means is that we are to reckon ourselves *judicially* dead to sin through the representatively all-inclusive atonement made on Calvary, which answered all the claim and penalty of the divine Law against us (but for a fuller dealing with this we must refer to our other volumes already mentioned).

What confusing mix-ups we get into when we persist in forcing Romans 6: 6 and Galatians 2: 20 to mean a simulated *subjective* death or dying to sin by a present identification with the Cross! Some years ago, in a well-known Christian magazine, an article appeared making keen accusations against this form of teaching on sanctification, the most serious charge being that it is considerably "Pelagian" (which it is not). There was a prompt answer by an able and gifted scholar who, however, sank knee-deep in the usual boggy theory. On the basis of Romans 6: 6, that "there on Calvary the old man of sin did actually die", he tells us that "we can *begin* actually to die with Jesus Christ". So instead of a death that is *over* (according to Paul) there is only a supposed death which now "*begins*" in the believer. Then comes this: "We *die* to the old nature—or old man—when we reckon ourselves dead indeed unto sin in *daily penitence*." So again there is a supposedly endless repetition of dyings instead of Paul's once-for-all (*ephapax*) past tense. One wonders why it did not occur to the learned writer that since "daily penitence" is daily sorrow for daily *sinning*, it evinces the very opposite of death to sin!

So eminently a theological expert is the author whom we are quoting that I cannot refrain from adding the following further excerpt, for it serves to show that if such able Bible students as he can be misled by this common but self-contradictory theory of experiential identification with the Cross, we need not wonder that others are beguiled (or bewildered) by it. Speaking of the supposed "two natures" in the believer, and the supposed death or dying of the "old" through our identification with the death of Christ, he says:

"This is a very difficult truth to state. It involves a tension, a duality almost. . . . The old man is still there *in all his malignity to the very end*. We have to die to him daily, to enter constantly into the victory of Calvary, or at the very last moment, even after a life of blameless service, he may work his most grievous mischief. . . . This dying to the old man and rising again to the new, in the power of the Word and the Spirit, is the process of sanctification. . . . Sin —the man of sin—is eradicated on the Cross. That is why we can be confident. Sin—the man of sin—*will* be eradicated in us. That is why we can look forward with hope. But here and now we live in the time between. We live in the passing age. We belong to that which is to come. To apply the term, 'eradication', to *this* life, except in an illustrative sense, is inappropriate and misleading, and may in certain cases be dangerous and harmful."

It is the same old yes-but-no penchant. The old man (wrongly supposed to be our "old nature") "did *actually* die", yet he is with us "in all his malignity to the very end"! We are to keep "dying daily" to sin, yet we never become dead to it, nor even *less* dead to it; an endless dying which is not really dying at all! The "man of sin" (alias our suppositionary "old nature") was "eradicated on the Cross", yet he is *not* eradicated *now*, but only "*will be* eradicated in us" in the life to come; for we now live in "the time between" that past eradication on Calvary and the inward eradication which is yet to be. So, after all, in the present interval our "old man", our evil self, neither is nor can be either "dead" or "eradicated"! Then why keep torturing Romans 6: 6 and Galatians 2: 20 to make them artificially mean something which, when once we have *forced* them to mean it, we immediately have to *deny*?

QUASI SCRIPTURAL ERROR

All our animadversions thus far, however, on this fond but futile phantasy of an inward death to sin by identification with Calvary, lead to our further and basic criticism that although it has an assumed Scripturalness it is in fact *un*scriptural. It is all the more alluring and deceiving, of course, *because* it seems to be such a spiritual-minded interpretation of Scripture.

One of its favourite props is Galatians 2: 20. I remember a large meeting in Manchester, England, years ago, in which Mr. J. H. Waite, a former treasurer of the Keswick Convention, appropriately remarked, "If I were asked to sum up as nearly as possible in one text of Scripture what the Keswick Convention is trying to emphasize, I should say Galatians 2: 20".

"I am crucified with Christ: nevertheless I live, yet not I, but Christ liveth in me; and the life which I now live in the flesh I live by the faith of the Son of God, who loved me, and gave Himself for me."

We may well be grateful to those convention platforms which have kept that vital truth reiteratedly to the fore. The trouble arises from the way Galatians 2: 20 is usually interpreted—or *mis*interpreted. Few texts have been oftener used at gatherings for the promotion of Scriptural holiness. It is frequently used as a proof text of the common "identification" theory. So we may fittingly use it, also, as a *test* text. It teaches identification with Christ in two ways: (1) the believer's crucifixion-death with Him, (2) the believer's resurrection-life with Him.

Identification in Death

"I am crucified with Christ," says Paul, according to our Authorized Version. On that basis the accepted identification idea teaches a present and inward crucifixion of the believer's so-called "self-life" or "old man" or "carnal nature". Some insist, quite consistently, that this means an inward *death* to sin, inasmuch as crucifixion is a putting to death. Others argue that it means a continual *dying* to sin, in which the "old nature" is pinioned to the Cross and thus rendered "inoperative" or put "out of action", but is never actually dead (obviously inconsistent in that it does not truly parallel with our Lord's crucifixion, which meant outright death, like every other crucifixion, not a never-ending dying). Reams of quotations might be given to show that such is the fashionable doctrine.

Yet it is patently a misuse of the text. To begin with, the Greek verb is not "I *am* crucified", but the perfect tense, "I have *been* crucified" (denoting an act already completed). So this crucifixion with Christ in Galatians 2: 20 is *not* a crucifixion happening in the present, neither is it a *continuous* crucifixion; it is a crucifixion completed and over.

Moreover, the preceding verse (19) plainly settles it that this death with Christ was *judicial*, not inward and spiritual. In it Paul says, "For I (*ego*, the whole man) died *TO THE LAW*"—which is immediately followed by our text, "I have been crucified with Christ" (i.e. by identification judicially in His death to the Law and its claim).

Then again, the whole context is about our *justification* (not sanctification) through this judicial (not experiential) identification with Christ. Paul rebukes Peter for his vacillation and says,

"We who are Jews by nature, and not sinners of the Gentiles, knowing that a man is not *JUSTIFIED* by works of the *LAW* but by faith in Jesus Christ, even we have believed in Jesus Christ that we might be *JUSTIFIED* by faith in Christ, and not by works of the *LAW:* for by the works of the *LAW* shall no flesh be *JUSTIFIED*. But if while we seek to be *JUSTIFIED* by Christ we ourselves also are found sinners, is therefore Christ the minister of sin? God forbid. If I build again the things which I destroyed, I make myself a *TRANS-GRESSOR*. For I through the *LAW* died [past and over] to the *LAW*, so that [having thus judicially died] I might live unto God. With Christ I have been crucified [completely, totally, judicially] nevertheless I live, yet no longer I, but Christ liveth in me, and that life which I now live in the flesh [i.e. in the body] I live by faith in the Son of God who loved me, and gave Himself for me. I do not frustrate the *GRACE* of God, for if *RIGHTEOUSNESS* is through the *LAW*, then Christ died for nought."

Surely then, if we honour the principle that a text must be interpreted in the light of its context, there can be no doubt that in Galatians 2: 20 the crucifixion with Christ is not experiential but solely *judicial*, having to do with the Law, transgression, and justification. It has nothing to do with a suppositionary *inward* death or process of *dying* to inbred depravity.

Identification in Life

Having spoken of this past and completed death with Christ in the judicial reckoning of God, Paul fittingly changes his verb into the present, continuous tense as he adds, "Nevertheless I live, yet not I, but Christ liveth in me . . ." This is indeed a present and continuous identification with our risen Lord. Here again, however, Galatians 2 : 20 has been misinterpreted. It has been supposed to mean that just as the so-called *"old* nature" or "old man" was crucified with Christ, so now the so-called *"new* nature" or "new man" *lives* in union with Christ. Yet that is not what Paul here teaches at all. He says that it was the whole "I" which was crucified with Christ (not just an "old nature") and that it is the whole "I" which now lives and is indwelt by the risen Lord. Those many who teach that it was the "old nature" which was crucified with Christ should in all consistency teach that it was the "old nature" which also was "raised with Him", for the only part which could be resurrected is the part which was crucified. The "new nature" (which according to theory is *not* sinful) could not be raised into newness of life, for *that* did not have to be crucified! It was the total "I" which died. It is the total "I" which lives. Surely this again shows that the death was judicial.

It is fatuous, of course, to say that any of us can be actually put on the cross of Christ; that our inner nature can somehow be transferred back through nineteen hundred years and fastened there with Him. To speak of such a shared crucifixion as going on now is just as wrong in its own way as the Roman Catholic doctrine of the Mass in which (strange superstition!) the bread and wine supposedly become the actual body and blood of our Lord as part of a "perpetual sacrifice". That Roman misconceit is utterly wrong because Scripture plainly declares, "In that He died, He died unto sin *once for all*"; "death hath no more dominion over Him" (Rom. 6: 9, 10). Again, *"Once for all* He offered Himself up", and "We are sanctified through the offering of the body of Jesus *once for all"* (Heb. 7: 27; 10: 10). And again, "Christ being raised from the dead *dieth no more"* (Rom. 6: 9). So, too, this teaching of a present, experiential crucifixion of the believer with Christ (when we really think it through) just as wrongly makes the cross of Christ a "perpetual" crucifixion. I know that many of our best known Evangelical leaders have long taught this fond delusion, but the sooner the distorted theory itself is dead and buried, the better.

Someone is sure to ask: What about the words, "I live, yet not I"? Do not the words, "yet not I", plainly mean that Paul was now dead in a way which was inwardly vivid to him? Yes, they do, but not in the way the usual holiness teaching tells us. Paul does not say, "I live, yet not the old nature", as though it were only a *part* of him which had now died. No, for in the words, "yet not I", the "I" is emphatic. It is the Greek *ego*, emphasizing that it was the total "I", the whole human person, which was now dead and gone. Paul simply cannot mean that he, the whole man, spirit, soul and body, had actually died by crucifixion and no longer existed. He therefore *must* mean that he, the whole man, had died in some relational or positional sense. That, in fact, is what he *does* mean, as the verse immediately preceding the text makes conclusive:

"For I (*ego*) through the Law *DIED TO THE LAW*, that I might live unto God."

Could anything be plainer? Here is no such fiction as the death of some inward *part* called the "old nature". He is talking about the relation of the total man to the violated Law. In the all-inclusive death of Christ, Paul now has died, and the appeased Law which said, "The soul that sinneth shall die", can exact no more; the penalty has been exacted. In the eyes of the divine Law the pre-conversion Saul was no more; he had been executed. Truly now could Paul say, "yet not I". Judicially that old "I" was gone for ever.

Do we need add more? Is not Paul's meaning unmistakable? The whole Adam race, in the judicial reckoning of God, was put away on that representative Cross: "All died in Him" (2 Cor. 5: 14). Although this present life on earth is probationary for all human beings as *individuals,* the Adam race as such is no longer on probation. Under different dispensations it had been tested, until it exhibited its final failure in the repudiation and crucifying of the sinless *Second* Adam. It had now been tried, sentenced, and put away in the judicial death of the great Sin-Bearer (even as Jesus Himself had said, "*Now* is the judgment of this world", i.e. Calvary). The final judgment of human *individuals* is still future, but in a legal sense the human *race* as such was dealt with in that profoundly meaningful Cross. That is why Paul adds, "Yea, even though we have known Christ after the flesh (i.e. as belonging to the Adam race) yet now we know even Him so no more". "Therefore if any man be in Christ there is a new creation; the old things are passed away; lo, all things have become new." That is exactly what had happened to Paul, and to which he gives testimony in Galatians 2: 20. As a human being now in union with the Head of the "new creation" He says, "Nevertheless I *live*"; but with a glance back at what he formerly was as a guilty member of the old Adam creation he adds, "Yet *not* I".

We have already noted some of the strange self-contradictions which are involved in the common theory that inward death to sin comes through a supposed experiential identification with the Cross. I do not wish superfluously to travel that ground again, yet I can scarcely resist this one further adversion to it, because it is the only way to show *some* dear believers (known as "deeply taught" in the Word) how wrong that theory is. I have before me an address on Galatians 2: 20 by one of the truest men of God whom I ever knew and loved. He became an outstanding leader, and often spoke at holiness conventions. I revered him too well to allow me now to name him as I here point out the well-meaning but peculiar contradictions in the following quotations from a printed address of his. Note particularly the capitalized words.

"You and I have been crucified with Christ; that is to say, we have *DIED* to sin. . . . It is that truth which brings the saint into the glorious experience of sanctification. . . . I am committed to the life of one who has *ACTUALLY DIED* to sin. Am I *PURPOSING* in the power of God to live the crucified life? . . . When such a decision has been made and such an attitude adopted, then it will not surprise us when we are slighted and overlooked; that is part of *DYING* to sin. We triumph over it by *DYING* to it as it comes to us."

Who can help asking: If we "actually died" to sin, how comes it that somehow we are still so alive to it that we have to keep "*dying*" to it? Some of us have grown so used to this form of holiness phraseology that the almost comical self-contradiction of it slips sleekly through our minds unopposed; yet the stark logic of reality is, that the necessity of our keep *dying* to sin implies a continuous aliveness to it which utterly refutes the prior statement that we "actually *died*" to it. But see further how this "dying to sin" becomes practically equated with a "dying to *self*".

"There will be plenty of occasions next week and the weeks after of *DYING TO SELF.* . . . They slight us . . . they persecute us . . . and they give us fresh occasion of *DYING TO SELF.* . . . If we have seen anything of the nature of *SELF,* I doubt not that some of us are willing to pay the price and reign in life over this *CRUEL SELF.*"

But we may well ask now: Since that so-called "old self" was crucified with Christ and "*died* to sin", which is the evil "*cruel* self" to which we are *now* to keep dying? Is it a *new* evil "self"? It must be, or else the "*old* self" is not dead at all! Or, if the "old self" *did* die, is there something badly wrong with my *remaining* "self"? If so, how can I myself *die* to my "self"?

"At Calvary there was something which perished and something which persisted. There was an 'I' which died, and an 'I' which lived. . . . The 'I' which died loves to be ministered unto: the 'I' which lives ministers unto others. The 'I' which died was a source; the 'I' which lives is a vessel. And when the old 'I' is renounced and put to death, then we are able to sing. . . ."

So it is the "old I" which is "renounced and put to death"— which supposedly happens in the believer's experience. Then why do we have to keep dying to the remaining "I" which lives on? I comment no further. This phantasmal notion of two "selves" or two "I"s or two "natures", and of a crucifixion which is *not* a crucifixion, and of a supposed inward death to sin which is *not* real death to sin at all, has worked more muddle and mystification than words will ever tell.

Some may wonder where this distorted "identification" theory originated. We can easily trace it back as far as the venerable John Wesley, with whom many assume that it began. John Wesley certainly gave it a very wide outreach, but its first post-Reformation progenitor was the Reverend Walter Marshall (1628–1680), whose large treatise known as *Marshall on Sanctification* has probably had a longer-lasting vogue than any other work on the subject. We know that Wesley prized it; and so have holiness teachers ever since. Of such a standard work let me speak with corresponding deference. In it there is much that is excellent; but it is away back there, in Marshall's classic, first published in 1692, that we find the "identification" theory elaborated and elucidated in the now familiar way. Wesley did not agree with Marshall that the "sin-principle" persists in the entirely sanctified, but otherwise, apparently, he "judged it to be an excellent book".

Much as we may prize and praise it, however, we cannot but marvel at the naïve unawareness of patent self-contradictions—which are inescapable in the theory of experiential co-crucifixion with Christ, and the death of a so-called "old nature" thereby. We are tempted to start quoting, but we resist, for we have already quoted perhaps more than enough to show how unscriptural the theory is.

Much as we esteem and love many of those who have taught the "identification" theory, we would earnestly advise Christian believers against it. Though it may sound attractively "spiritual" it is not truly Scriptural; and those who presume to act upon it are exercising, not faith, but credulity.

Dear Christian believer, be assured of this: the Calvary and high priestly ministry of our glorious Lord cover all that which needed to be done *FOR* you; but it is the Holy Spirit alone who, as the Executive of our divine Saviour, does all that is needed to be done *IN* you. Of course, the Holy Spirit is the "Spirit of *Christ*"; therefore all that the Spirit does within us is, in that sense, our Lord Himself at work in us. What the Scriptures *really* teach as the way of inwrought sanctification is not a crucifixion of some imagined "old man" inside us, but the thorough "renewing of our mind" unto holiness by the Holy Spirit. Let this be axiomatic in all your thinking about sanctification: Our Lord Jesus, through His atoning death, is the *PROCURING CAUSE* of our sanctification. The Holy Spirit, by whom Christ indwells us, is the *EFFECTING AGENT* in our sanctification. Read Weymouth's rendering of Romans 12: 2 again, and then pray that the wonderful inward renewing which it pledges may be made real in you; for that is truly *inwrought sanctification*.

"I plead with you therefore, brethren, by the compassion of God, to present all your faculties to Him as a living and holy sacrifice to Him—a spiritual mode of worship. And do not conform to the present age, but be *TRANSFORMED BY THE ENTIRE RENEWAL OF YOUR MINDS,* so that you may learn by experience what God's will is, namely, all that is good and acceptable to Him, and perfect."

Grasp it firmly: sanctification is made *possible* solely and wholly through the Cross of our dear Lord. It is made *actual* within us by the infilling of the Holy Spirit, the Spirit of Christ. That infilling by the Holy Spirit is received through consecration and faith: and *that* is what effects inwrought sanctification.

SANCTIFICATION AND THE SELF

"It will be an ill day when our brethren take to bragging and boasting, and call it 'testimony to the higher life.' We trust that holiness will be more than ever the aim of believers, but not the boastful holiness which has deluded some of the excellent of the earth into vainglory, and under which their firmest friends shudder for them."

C. H. Spurgeon.

"If someone had drawn Tennyson's notice to the fact that, in the poem of dedication he had written to the gracious lady who was his wife, *four* lines were about her, and the other *nine* about himself, he would probably have been astonished. A sense of self-importance is myopic: it blinds as it grows."

W. E. Sangster.

SANCTIFICATION AND THE SELF

PERHAPS the subtlest of all errors concerning sanctification are those which concern "the *self*"; and they are just as common as they are subtle.

With most of us, at the time of our conversion, the uppermost concern of our minds is salvation from the guilt and penalty of our *sins*. The Cross of Christ suddenly becomes a mighty wonder to us. We see the Son of God there, making vicarious atonement; and with unutterable relief we appropriate through Him "the forgiveness of *sins*". Later, a more persistent problem scourges us: the problem of innate *sin*. We still rejoice in sins forgiven, yet at the same time we are groaning in bondage to "sin that dwelleth in me". Try as we will, we cannot master the long-entrenched foe, and we cry out with the "wretched man" of Romans 7, "Who shall deliver me?" Still later, even though we may have grasped the Scriptural way of dealing with "sin that dwelleth in me", there is an even deeper and subtler problem: the problem of the *self*. That famous evangelist, D. L. Moody, said, "The man who has given me more trouble than any other is D. L. Moody". His words twang an answering vibration in most of us.

> Allurings outside me; responses within;
> What subtle collusions betray me to sin!
> Yet somehow involved in each fall, I descry
> That innermost problem: the self that is "I".

How are we to deal with that problematical "self"? A very common idea is that it must be "crucified". According to not a few preachers and writers, sanctification consists in the eradication or at least the subjugation of the self. Indeed, one of the commonest ideas is that the way of rescue from the tyranny of sin is the ousting or crippling of the so-called "self-life". For instance, a certain hymn tells us,

> There is a foe whose hidden power
> The Christian well may fear;
> More subtle far than inbred sin,
> And to the heart more dear:

> It is the power of selfishness,
> The proud and wilful "I";
> And ere my Lord can live in me
> My very *SELF* must die.

Or take the following quotation: "Not till the 'self' has been crucified with Christ and buried with Him can we rightly reckon ourselves to have been raised with Him in 'the power of His resurrection'." One of my best-loved devotional authors, the late F. B. Meyer, says, "The self-life is our greatest struggle. . . . It is the ego-bias which spoils the music of our lives. . . . But there is deliverance: our self-life has been nailed to the Saviour's Cross. . . . We must regard ourselves as dead to sin and *self*."

Misleading Ambiguity

Now all such reference to the "self" is either misleadingly *ambiguous*, or else it is definitely *erroneous*. When I say that it is often "ambiguous", I mean that again and again it is used (as in the foregoing quotations) as being synonymous with "the *flesh*". When preachers and books on holiness insist that the "self" must die, in nine cases out of ten they mean that "the *flesh*" must be put to death. The difference between the "self" and the "flesh" is, that the "self" is the basic human *ego* or person, including both good and evil heredity, whereas the "flesh" is a Paulinism meaning distinctively the *animal and selfish* propensities inhering in us. Death of the "self" would be nothing less than the annihilation of the thinking human ego itself. Therefore the New Testament nowhere teaches such a contrariety as the crucifixion or death of the *self*; but it certainly does teach the crucifixion of the *flesh*—"They that are Christ's have crucified the *flesh* [not the 'self'] with the affections and lusts" (Gal. 5: 24); and it also teaches that we are to "mortify" (or put to death) the "doings" of the flesh through the human *body* (Rom. 8: 13).

We need to be wary and discriminating, therefore, whenever we see that word, "self", used in connection with Christian sanctification. Either it should be replaced by Paul's figurative expression, "the flesh", or by some such word as "self*ism*", or "selfishness", or "self-centredness". Its ambiguous use has brought false hope or misunderstanding to many. One of my favourite hymns begins,

> My Saviour, Thou has offered rest;
>   Oh, give it then to me:
> The rest of *ceasing from myself*,
>   To find my all in Thee.

But the Scripture nowhere promises any such fictitious rest as a cessation from my very self! To presume that it does only leads to self-delusion.

> This cruel self, oh, how it strives,
>   And works within my breast,
> To come between Thee and my soul,
>   And keep me back from rest!

But how *can* the self "come between" Christ and "my soul" when the self *is* the soul? All the way through such verses the author does not mean the basic human self at all, even though he uses the *word*, "self"; he means those selfish and animal propensities within us which Paul collectively calls "the flesh". So long as we understand the word, "self", to mean the various movings of self*ism*, i.e. self-ambition, self-wisdom, self-seeking, self-conceit, self-pity, and so on, such hymns, prayers, longings are truly spiritual and intelligent; but to mean by it one's very "self" is to entertain an illusion.

As a matter of preciseness, the term, "self", is not even good English. It is a truncated form of the noun, "selfishness", and is of only late appearance. It is not Biblical. Nowhere in Scripture do we find such statements as are now common in conferences on the deeper Christian life—for instance, "the self-life must be slain"; "the self-life is the flesh"; "the self is the old nature"; "in the self is nothing but sin". The Bible is misrepresented by such clichés; for it everywhere recognises that in the basic human self there is both *good* and bad. It carefully *distinguishes* between the self and "the flesh", e.g. in Romans 7: 18, where Paul says, "For I know that in me, that is, in my *flesh*, dwelleth no good thing . . . but with the *mind* [the true self] I serve the law of God". Let it be settled once for all in our minds: the "self" is not identical with the "flesh". The "flesh" is only one *aspect* of the self. Sanctification consists, not in a supposed eradication or subjugation of the self, but in the *sublimation* of it through a renewing immersion in the Holy Spirit. Extinction of the self is nowhere taught in our New Testament; but the "transformation" of it (Greek: *metamorphosis*) is: see Romans 12: 2; 2 Corinthians 3: 18; Ephesians 4: 23.

An Extravaganza of Mysticism

But wrapped up in this problem of the so-called "self" there are other and more peculiar errors which stem from a hyper-introspective type of spirituality. Whenever we become "spiritual" beyond what Scripture teaches, faith degenerates into presumption; our theory of sanctification lifts us away from solid footing, and has us treading clouds of lofty imagination, until sooner or later we suddenly find ourselves let down into the bogs of disillusionment. Many seekers after holiness have been impeded, even tortured, by the teaching that *self is sin*. They and their teachers have committed the fallacy of making the disease and the patient identical. They have assumed that because the patient *has* a disease, the patient *is* the disease! But what Gospel can save me if my very ego is itself *sin*? If I am such a being, the only way to save me is to deprive me of *being*. Nirvana is the goal!

> Self must be slain by self-annihilation,
> The nearer nothing, so much more divine.

Thank God, the New Testament teaches no such Christianized Buddhism! Yet in subtle disguise, that is just what various forms of Christian mysticism have taught—often with all too wide an acceptance. True Christianity is essentially spiritually-minded, but that does not make all *forms* of spiritual-mindedness truly Christian. There can be a spirituality, an inwardness, which is self-occupied, introversive, and contemplative for its own sake rather than for outgoing good to others. Far too much of that is found in *mysticism*. Indeed, therein lies its appeal. In days past, to many a heart in quest of holiness, mysticism has seemed a healthy protest of true Protestantism against the sacerdotalism of the Roman Catholic Church; and in more recent days it has seemed a true reaction against the formalism and showy externalism which have considerably disfigured some Protestant denominations.

For instance, the famous Quietist, Madame Guyon, who is widely extolled as one of the spiritually élite to be emulated, has little in common with *evangelical* Protestantism beyond her devout emphasis on the *inwardness* of the Christian religion. To us evangelical believers the New Testament clearly teaches that salvation is by faith; not by works. Madame Guyon also *seems* to oppose faith to works, but it is only faith as against outward observances such as Rome teaches. To us evangelical believers, holiness is a *result* of communion with God, whereas with Madame Guyon holiness is a *prerequisite* to communion with God. As Professor Thomas Upham, one of her admirers, says, she suspended "acceptance with God", on "inward disposition". That wonderful keystone in the arch of Gospel truth—salvation by faith alone, in the finished work of Calvary, was unknown to her. Along with other Quietists, to her the soul that is filled with God is the soul that is emptied of *itself*. The great thing is to "nought" oneself. That is not peculiar to the Quietists; it is a main characteristic of all mysticism. Eckhart voices it when he says, "A man shall become as truly poor and as free from his creature will as he was when he was born. . . . He alone hath true spiritual poverty who wills nothing, knows nothing, desires nothing." It is this complete voiding of the soul, of the *self*, which (supposedly) perfects communion with God.

Some of the morbid inanities seriously indulged by various mystics, in their pathetic passion to be freed from self and lost in God, are grimly comical to many of us who are less "spiritual". Swester Katrei (Sister Katherine) of Strasbourg has it that "not even the desire for heaven" should be allowed to disturb the utter passivity of the soul. We are told that "on one occasion she became cataleptic, and was being carried to burial for dead. Her confessor, just in time, discovered that it was a trance instead of death, and awoke her. Katherine exclaimed, 'Now I am satisfied, for I have been dead all through.' " Another "Friend of God" who (supposedly) so fully attained the coveted utter indifference that "through the power of love" he "became without [i.e. *free* from] love", heard a voice say to him, "Permit Me, my beloved child, to share in thee, and with thee, all the riches of My divinity; all the passionate love of My humanity; all the joys of the Holy Spirit"; to which the "friend of God" replied, "Yes, Lord, I permit Thee, on condition that Thou alone shalt enjoy it, and not I"!

Such mysticism, just as truly as Pantheism, destroys all sense of separate personality. As B. B. Warfield puts it, what seem to be human individualities are "mere momentary wavelets on the bosom of the deep of being". And underneath *all* such mysticism is the fundamental error that human nature is itself *sin*. The mystic's idea of salvation is not that the human self must be saved from *sin*, so much as that man must be saved from *himself*, thus to be lifted to a higher purity and oneness with God than man possessed even in his original purity. Human nature may climb *above itself* into absorption with the Divine. This is the lure of the hyper-spiritual. It seems to open up heights of possibility which exalt human nature, but in reality it irreverently dishonours it by teaching that human nature has to be saved from the ugliness which is *itself*.

Under the influence of such Mysticism the merely natural has been equated with degradation. Human hearts have sighed, groaned, fasted, prayed, and exhausted themselves in intense vigils to be saved from their very *selves* as the only way to be saved from sin. The quest has been, not merely a purified nature, but a *superior* nature, which has led to the mystic's characteristic contempt for our common humanhood. To the Quietists and others the only sanctification is the extinction of the self. We must die to everything which we love for self-sake, even the desire for salvation or virtue, or anything, until, like a river reaching the ocean, the soul loses its own powers and capacities in an immensity beyond itself. Or, in the words of Catherine of Genoa, "God was made man that He might make men God". Madame Guyon herself says, "The soul is not merely hidden in God, but has in God become God". Or again, much nearer to our own time, Upham says, "Perhaps the most decisive mark of the truly crucified man is, that he is crucified to holiness itself".

Now in all this—and far more of it persists today than many think—there is an ironic cheating the soul of the very blessing which it most achingly covets, namely, *fellowship with God*. What is sought in mysticism, is not just likeness to God, but *coalescence* with Him; not just conformity to Him, but *identity* with Him. Yet unless we retain separate individuality of soul, God and we lose that loveliest of all purposes for which He created us, that is, *divine fellowship with other beings*. The Scripture teaches no such mystical self-inhibition to the point of personal nihility. It does not even go so far as to teach (as some of our hymns do) that the Christian's *will* is to be "lost" in God's: it teaches that the heart and will are to become *one* with God's in the sense of our *voluntarily* desiring and willing only what our benign Creator-Father Himself desires and wills for us.

However painfully we are plagued by the obstinate puzzle of the so-called "self", let none of us be drawn into the spider's web of mysticism! Holiness, other than being the abolition of self, is the *assertion* of it in its purest and highest expression of the divine image. It was when the prodigal *"came to himself"* (Luke 15: 17) that he did the right thing: he came back to the Father. Up to that point he had listened to "the *flesh*", which eventually led him down to the husks; but when he listened to his true *self* he learned the first step to restored sonship and fellowship with the Father. Nowhere in the Bible do we find prayers for annihilation or for absorption into God. Jeremiah prayed, "O Lord, correct me, but with judgment; not in Thine anger, *lest* Thou bring me to *nothing*". Paul becomes similarly significant when he says, *not* "By the grace of God I am now *nothing*", but, "By the grace of God I am what *I am*" (1 Cor. 15: 10). Let us learn it firmly and finally: the sanctification to which our New Testament calls us is neither the cancellation of the self through crucifixion nor its gradual vaporization into infinite divinity, but its individual *renewal* by the Holy Spirit into *inwrought* personal holiness.

A *"Higher Life"* Fallacy

Coming "nearer home" to many of us, however, this mystical "spirituality" finds common expression today in a certain way of teaching that *"Christ is our life"* (Col. 3: 4). It is focalized in the chorus of a well-known hymn:

> Oh, to be saved from *myself*, dear Lord!
> Oh, to be *lost in Thee*!
> Oh, that it may be *no more "I"*,
> But Christ who lives in me!

The teaching is, that the believer's self is *replaced* by Christ. Years ago, as a young Christian, I came under the influence of persuasive pamphlets giving this teaching. Let me quote:

"The simple fact is, that whenever a life which trusts Christ as Saviour is completely surrendered to Christ as Master, Christ is ready then to take complete control of that life, and at once to fill it with Himself. . . . When we surrender and trust completely, we die to self; and Christ can and does *literally replace our self with Himself*. Thus it is no longer we that live, but Christ . . . literally fills our whole being with Himself in actual, personal presence; and He does this not as a figure of speech, but just as literally as that we fill our clothes with ourselves."

We are "to enter upon the very life of God; to be 'as He is' even in this world" (1 John 4: 17). Instead of fighting temptation, we "simply let Christ dispose of it, while we stand by like on-lookers". Giving his own testimony, the above-quoted author says in another pamphlet:

"At last I realized that Jesus Christ was actually and literally within me; and even more than that: that He had constituted Himself my very being . . . my body, mind, soul, and spirit. . . . My body was His, my mind His, my Spirit His; and not merely His, but literally a part of Him. . . . Jesus Christ had constituted Himself my life—not as a figure of speech, remember, but as a literal, actual fact, as literal as the fact that a certain tree has been made into this desk on which my hand rests."

Such teaching, fantastic though it is, has allured thousands (and still does) by its seemingly penetrating spirituality. It has made almost mesmeric appeal to spiritually minded believers longing to know the secret of inward holiness and victory over self. Through facile pens and persuasive lips, it has had wide acceptance. It has brought thousands together in widely adver-tized conventions. It has also engendered in too many of its disciples a spiritual superiority-complex which is the very opposite of the truly Christlike life. Its well-meaning original spokesmen, Charles G. Trumbull, Hannah Whitall Smith, W. E. Board-man, and others,[1] are no longer with us, but their "victorious life" and "higher life" vagaries still are. Out they come, again and again, in many an address today at Conferences for the pro-motion of Christian holiness, punctuated by the usual clichés: we must "die to the self"; "the self in us must be slain"; "the self-life and the Christ-life cannot dwell together"; we must be "emptied of self if we are to be filled with Christ".

Whether some of the present sponsors of this plausible teach-ing are alive to the logical implications of their phraseology I rather doubt; but if there is one subject more than another on which our terminology needs to be accurate and free from exag-geration it is this sacred, sensitive matter of personal holiness. Look back over those pamphlet quotations which we have just submitted: they are not only a fevered overstraining of Scripture; they teach nothing less than an *extinction* of our individual per-sonality. "When we surrender and trust completely", the first

---

[1] All excellent in exemplary Christian character and in other ways.

says, "we die to self; and Christ can and does literally *replace* our self with Himself". So apparently not even the *suffusion* of the self by Christ is enough; there is a *substitution* of the self by Christ!

A widely influential tract, *The Christ Life*, says, "God seemed to speak to me so sweetly, saying, 'Never mind, my child, *you* have nothing: but I *am* perfect Power, I am perfect Love, I am Faith, I am your Life, I am the preparation for the blessing, and then I am the Blessing too. I am all, within and without, and all forever.' " The author adds: "It is just having 'the faith of God' (Mark 11: 22 margin)," by which he turns the Greek objective genitive round to mean that the faith which (supposedly) *God* has takes the place of *my* faith in God. That such is his meaning is at once confirmed by his treating the objective genitive in Galatians 2: 20 in just the same way ("The life which I now live, I live by the faith of the Son of God"). He next says, "It is not *your* faith. You have no faith in you, any more than you have life or anything else in you. . . . You have to take His faith as well as His life and healing, and have simply to say, 'I live by the faith of the Son of God'. . . . It is simply Christ alone."

I go back to Trumbull's assertion: "I realized that Jesus Christ . . . had constituted Himself my very being." Amazingly enough, he immediately tacks on to that the parenthetical note ("save only my power to resist Him"). But if Christ has "constituted Himself my very being . . . my body, mind, soul, and spirit", what can there be *left* to "resist" Him? Any resistance must be Christ resisting Himself! In reality, that parenthesis means that Christ replaces everything *except* my free will—which in turn means that Christ has not replaced me at all!

The teaching is just as self-contradicting as it is hyper-spiritual and exegetically untenable. We will not linger longer over it, except to add a final word of warning against it. As a sample of the way in which it has been put over to the Christian public, I quote from an article by Trumbull in a back number of *The Sunday School Times*. "Christ is living the victorious life today; and Christ is your life. Therefore stop trying. Let Him do it all. Your effort or trying had nothing to do with the salvation which you have in Christ: in exactly the same way your effort and trying can have nothing to do with the complete victory which Christ alone has achieved for you and can steadily achieve in you."

How attractive and Christ-honouring this "let *Him* do it *all*" Gospel sounds! But there are three facts which utterly disqualify it. (1) It is not truly Scriptural; (2) It simply does not work out in experience; (3) Mr. Trumbull himself says, "God can save no man unless that man does his part toward salvation". Man's part (he says) is to "receive", and that is true, but it is far from the whole truth. There is to be yielding, self-disciplining, striving against temptation, striving in prayer. According to Paul, the very fact that "it is God which worketh in you both to will and to do of His good pleasure" is the reason why we are to "*work out your* own salvation" (Phil. 2: 12, 13).

Any renewal which may be wrought within the moral nature of the Christian believer *must* be exclusively the work of the Holy Spirit, for self cannot change self; but no holiness ever inwrought by the Holy Spirit removes the need for co-operative human activity. Let there be prayerlessness or carelessness, and we lose the blessing. There is a true sense in which divinely inwrought holiness is to be *completed* by human response. As Paul says, in 2 Corinthians 7: 1, "Let us cleanse *ourselves* from all uncleanness of the flesh and spirit, *completing* holiness in the fear of God". Or, again, "If a man therefore cleanse *himself* from these, he shall be a vessel unto honour, sanctified . . ." (2 Tim. 2: 21).

As we have said earlier, our dear Lord fights our battles *with* us, but never *instead* of us. There is no need for *Him* to gain new victories, for through the once-for-all victory of His Cross and resurrection, all foes are forever "beneath Him". What He now designs is *our* victory in union with Himself. If (as is theorized) Christ now lives *instead* of me, all the temptations which come ostensibly to me *miss* me (for I am no longer there) and present themselves to Christ, on whom, however, they are completely wasted, as *He* has no response whatever. It robs me of all the benefits of self-discipline, of all union with Christ in moral conquest, and of all rejoicing in victory "through Christ which strengtheneth *me*" (Phil. 4: 13). It also leaves me with the strange puzzle: if Christ in me now lives *instead* of me, why do all the temptations which come to *Him* because of His having replaced me, keep hurting *me*?

We would warn everyone who chances on these pages: Beware just as wakefully against hyper-spiritual extremisms as against theological heresies. They may not tamper with foundational verities of the Faith, but they cause untold havoc among sincere

Evangelicals. I think the following culling from J. R. Miller is
well worth pondering.

"There are those who sigh for holiness and beauty of character,
but they are not willing to pay the price. They sing 'More holiness
give me,' and dream of some lofty spiritual attainment, some transfiguration, but they are not willing to endure the toils, fight the battles,
and make the self-sacrifices necessary to win these celestial heights.
They would make prayer a substitute for effort, for struggle, for the
crucifying of the flesh. They want a larger spiritual inheritance, but
they have no thought of taking it in primeval forests which their own
hands must cut down.

"The truth is, however, that God gives us our inheritance just as
He gave Joseph's lot to him. Our promised land has to be won, every
inch of it. And each one must win his own personal portion. No one
can win the inheritance for any other. You must conquer your own
temptations—your dearest friend by your side cannot overcome them
for you. You must train your own faith. You must cultivate your
own heart-life. You must learn patience, gentleness, and all the
lessons of love for yourself. No one can give you any Christian
grace. . . . Even God cannot give us holiness, peace, and all the
results of victorious living, without struggle, battle, or self-denial
upon our own part."

Let us treasure more than ever the truth of Galatians 2 : 20,
"Christ liveth in me" ; but let us not strain it into meaning "Christ
liveth *instead* of me". Dear Christian, even our Lord Jesus cannot live your life *for* you, though, thank God, He is ever *with* you
and *within* you. Your victory over sin must be your own. If it is
Christ's only, and *not* your own, then it is artificial, not real ; you
have not been made morally strong enough to win ; you have been
made merely negative ; your holiness is false ; you yourself are
not really changed at all. But, according to Scripture, *you* are
meant to win *through* Christ. That kind of victory develops holy
character in yourself, but gives all the ultimate glory to Christ.
Our true motto is Philippians 4 : 13, "I CAN . . . THROUGH
CHRIST". That, and that alone, is my true secret of moral and
spiritual victory.

SOME FINAL REFLECTIONS

"It is not an accident that the men who have most given themselves to the slavish observance of duty—Stoics, Pharisees, ascetic monks and Puritans—are, for the most part, hard and cheerless souls. They seem to have been quarried, not born. Noble and austerely splendid as their best types unquestionably are, they fail in one of the chief tests of true sanctity, and prove that this is a false path for us. They are not *happy*, and the flaw is fatal. They could not pray with George MacDonald, 'Lord, make my spirit good and *gay*'. They do not recognize joy as a necessary mark of the saint, and they would make all life not merely serious (which, of course, it is) but solemn (which it need not be)."

W. E. Sangster.

SOME FINAL REFLECTIONS

THE foregoing chapters have presented (in part one), and defended (in part two) the truth that sanctification, as a divinely inwrought *renewal*, is a Scripturally taught and provenly experienced *reality*. The beginning of it in a Christian's experience occurs together with conversion, but usually its deeper meaning is not grasped or entered into until considerably later. Alas, thousands of truly regenerated Christian believers know little if anything of it throughout their days on earth. Many are never taught it through the public ministry of the Word. Others have such a vague idea of it that they never concentratedly seek it. Still others, although they grasp the Scripturalness of it, allow earthly considerations to keep them from it.

In this addendum chapter I wish to gather up the main emphases of this book in some final reflections. If experiential sanctification is possible *at* conversion, it is certainly appropriable any time onwards *from* conversion. Yet it is not *identical* with conversion, any more than Israel's coming out of Egypt was identical with Israel's later entering into Canaan. The possessing of Canaan was *potentially* included in the salvation which freed Israel from Egypt, yet it was something which had to be appropriated *later*. All Christians, from soon after their conversion onwards, should be pointed to this intended, wonderful *complement* of conversion —the experience of a divinely inwrought *sanctification*.

That leads me to the first of my parting reflections. The sanctification of the believer's nature is *a definite work of the Holy Spirit* which must not be confused with anything which we ourselves can do. It is not something which can be developed by our own intensive cultivation of the spiritual life. There may be a real place for soul-culture; but inward sanctification is not to be confused with any such self-generated improvement of character. Nor is it only our self-yieldedness to Christ. It is specifically a *work of God* in response to consecration and faith, in which He *renews* the believer's moral nature in all its propensies, motives,

desires and inclinations. There is a place for godly human resolution about many things in the Christian life; but not all the fixed
resolutions of a life-time can bring about what only *God* can effect
in our nature. We are no more *sanctified* by resolves than we are
justified by resolves. What happens in inwrought sanctification is
supernatural. If this were not so, sanctification would not be a
vital concern; but inward sanctification *is* a post-conversion
miracle of renewal, and therefore it *is* vital.

Our second reflection is this: We must not confuse the *experience* of sanctification with merely appreciating the *doctrine*
of sanctification. To assent that a theory of holiness is true, or
even eagerly to enjoy it intellectually, is very different from living
in the transforming *experience* of it. I have known not a few
Christian persons who loved holiness meetings—loved to hear the
preaching of it; loved to sing hymns about it; and loved to speak
the language of it, who quite plainly had no vital experience of it.
I have seen them nodding their heads approvingly as the life in
Canaan was expounded, yet they were nodding approval from
the wrong side of the Jordan. They had not "gone up" and "possessed". I would say to all: Beware of thinking you are *there*
simply because you believe in the *doctrine* of it.

Third, inwrought sanctification *itself* is a deep-going renewal
of all the desires, impulses, proclivities and motives of the believer's moral nature, so that now the dominant inclination of
mind and heart is toward the holy. Along with this there may
be periodic "enduements" of the Holy Spirit for special service;
but sanctification itself is to be distinguished from all such, inasmuch as it is a *continuous* inward renewing by the Divine Spirit,
with a view to the transfiguration of *character*.

Again, this state of sanctification cannot be captured by attempt-
ing to copy the experience of *others*. Younger Christians often
pray for, and sometimes try hard to simulate, the experience of
admired older believers who testify to vivid enjoyments of sanctification. Others perhaps will read the biography of some outstanding saint, and then exclaim, "Yes, I knew there was an
experience like that; and that is what I want". Such attempted
emulations are a mistake. The Holy Spirit is just as original as
He is sovereign. Human experiencing of inwrought sanctification differs endlessly—just as it does in conversion. Dear Christian, if you are seeking this "fulness of the blessing" (as Paul
calls it) do not decide in advance what it will be like, or how

it will register itself in your consciousness. Leave that to the Holy Spirit. *Your* "experience" probably will not coincide in detail with any other.

That leads, of course, to our next advice, which is: Distinguish between the blessing and its *accompaniments*. Years ago, when, as a young believer, I myself was earnestly seeking the blessing of a cleansed and Spirit-filled heart, I began to think my much praying was all in vain because there came no volcanic eruption of ecstatic emotion such as many others had reportedly experienced at the crisis-point of entering into the blessing. I mistakenly concluded that the blessing itself was being withholden from me since such expected *accompaniments* of it never came; and at length I wearily gave up seeking. How many others have been set back by similar misunderstanding and discouragement! When once we have really yielded our all to Christ, we need not wait for tumults of emotional evidence; we may *count* on Him to sanctify the fully-yielded vessel, leaving to *Him* whatever way He chooses to make it *real* to us.

To that we must add: Be clear as to the part *faith* plays in the effecting of sanctification within us. When we say that sanctification comes through faith we do not mean that faith is the effecting *agent* of it, but only that it is the receptive *means* by which we appropriate what God has provided for us in Christ, and what He does within us by the power of the Holy Spirit.

Also, while we are mentioning the relation of *faith* to sanctification, we may well insert this comment on the conjunction of faith and *effort* in sanctification. All that is divinely wrought within us must obviously be received by faith, inasmuch as it is a work beyond our own power. Yet on the human side there is to be perseverence in *prayer*, which is one of the means through which communion with Christ and absorption of His communicated life are maintained. There is also to be (in dependence on Him) continual resistance of temptation; continual determination not to allow anything to come between us and the will of God; continual endeavour to fulfil all the teachings and admonishings of the written Word; continual guarding against wrong ambition or inordinate desire. All this, and more indeed, is necessary on the human side (all in dependence on Christ, of course); for while none of it in itself can *effect* inward sanctification, *all* of it is necessary if the renewing work of the Holy Spirit within us is not to be impeded.

This reference to vigil on our own part may serve as a reminder that entire sanctification is never a state in which we are no longer beset by *temptation,* or in which we have no further responsiveness or susceptibility to sinful *beguilement.* It is not a state in which we no longer need the imparted grace and power of Christ to keep us from sin. On the contrary, we need more grace and power than ever (and we find it more *real* than ever) to preserve us in the sweet experience of such mind-elevating spiritual fulness. Nor is sanctification a fixed state or level which leaves no room or need for further *progress* in holiness. Nay, it is sanctification which makes such progress possible. There is a true sense in which, according to Hebrews 2: 10, and 5: 8, 9, even the sinless "Captain of our salvation" was "perfected" as such through "sufferings" and "obedience".

Furthermore, let us always remember that the truest test as to whether we are entirely sanctified is not feelings but *motives*; not visitations of mental ecstasy, but a heart which loves the will of God, whatever the cost, and which feels sincere concern to help others. Any doting on subjective luxuries of emotion is not practical sanctification, but a spurious diversion. When the heart truly loves God above the dearest Isaac in our life, we *know* it; and therein is the deepest evidence of the Holy Spirit's work within us. Emotional attestations there assuredly may be, but they are the efflorescences rather than the essential reality of character-sanctification.

Dear Christian believer, have no doubt that the New Testament calls you to entire sanctification *now.* Nowhere in Scripture is the death of the body spoken of as that which terminates sin in the saints, despite the fact that believers are often consoled by being told that death will eventually bring them this liberation. If death were such a boon, would none of the inspired writers have at least noticed the fact? Death, in itself, has no such sanctifying power. Whether in this present life or in the larger life beyond, *any* sanctifying change wrought within us is exclusively the gracious work of the divine Spirit; and the unmistakable teaching of the New Testament (as our earlier pages have shown) is that our entire sanctification is available *now,* through Christ, by the infilling Holy Spirit.

Finally, think again what sanctification means to one's spiritual life, and how we may enter into the rich blessing of it. Going with the Spirit's renovation of all the desires, tempers, proclivities, preferences and responses of the mind, there is His inward *witness* to our heavenly sonship in Christ, and to our constant acceptance at the heavenly throne. There is an accompanying deeper realization of His ministry as the ever-indwelling *Paraclete*, strengthening, comforting, enlightening, interpreting, guiding, energising. There is an enlargement of our spiritual capacities, and an endowing with spiritual gifts; and there are successive enduements for Christian witness or other service. There gradually develops a new Christ-consciousness, a Christ-communicativeness, a new atmospheric around the consecrated personality.

Those are some of the sure concommitants of true sanctification; but in the words of 1 Kings 10: 7, "the half was never told". And do these words of mine chance to be read by some believer "hungering and thirsting" after holiness? Our Lord says of such, "They shall be filled". Not only so; He says that the "hunger and thirst" is itself "blessed"—for it indicates the preparatory influence of the Holy Spirit within the heart, inducing holy *desire*. From that point, then, dear disciple, go forward. You are on sure ground as you keep close to the New Testament and the divine promise given in it. "This is the will of God, even your sanctification" (1 Thess. 4: 3). "Christ is made unto us . . . sanctification" (1 Cor. 1: 30). "Faithful is He who calleth you [to this entire sanctification] who also will do it" (1 Thess. 5: 24).

The way in, as we have repeated and emphasized in our earlier chapters, is complete *self-yielding* to Christ, accompanied by simple but undaunted *faith to receive*. We can never possess what God has not promised; but when a blessing is vouchsafed as clearly as inward sanctification is in the New Testament, we need not hesitate to believe that God will make it real, if we implement the conditions of receiving. Yet even where the divine promise is clear, faith can never lay hold of it while there is refusal or neglect to surrender our *all* to Christ. Defective consecration paralyses the hand of faith. Have we not all found it so? Incomplete yielding means incomplete trust in Christ; therefore we find ourselves incapable of confidently "laying hold" of the proffered blessing. On the other hand, when once our self-yielding is unreserved, eager, utter, the frustrating fetters suddenly fall away from our faith, and appropriation becomes just as easy as it has hitherto been elusive.

Dear Christian, there is no spiritual problem, no hereditary bias, which inwrought sanctification cannot effectually deal with, so that you may live a life of continuous moral victory. Take the following quotation from Finney, which is as verifiable as it is vigorous.

"The Gospel, as a matter of fact, has often, not only temporarily, but permanently and perfectly, overcome every form of sin in different individuals. Who has not seen the most beastly lusts, drunkenness, lasciviousness, and every kind of abomination, long indulged and fully ripe, entirely and forever slain by the power of the grace of God? . . . In multitudes of cases, even when the appetite has not been entirely slain, the will has been endowed with abundant and abiding efficiency effectually to control it. If the most inveterate habits of sin, and even those that involve physical consequences, and have deeply debased the physical constitution, and rendered it a source of overpowering temptation to the mind, can be, and often have been, utterly broken up, and forever slain by the grace of God, why should it be doubted, that by the same grace a man can triumph over all sin, and that forever?"

If you are persuaded that such sanctification is the greatest thing that can happen to you this side of heaven, seek it with all your heart. Get alone with God, with your Lord and Saviour, with the Holy Spirit who is your divine Renewer; ask for imparted grace to yield yourself fully to the divine possession, for time and eternity; and really *do* thus yield yourself. Mark the date, the hour, the moment. Count it done. Do not start running round to the back of your own mind to see if you are really sincere, or to see if you are really meaning it. As a matter of *will* and of deep *desire,* utter your very heart to your all-knowing Lord. *Mean* it, and *do* it; and then count it *done.* You have at last given Him your whole being, and you are not going to be any longer self-cheated by waiting for emotional registrations, or by doubting your own deepest intention. If the subtle enemy can harass you into a futile round of repeatedly doing it and *doubting* it, he will mock you into incurable chaos; but you can beat him if you thoughtfully *will* to do it once for all; then deliberately *do* it; then count it *settled.*

What if you soon afterward fall into some sin of thought or word or deed? Does that *cancel* your solemn, utter yielding of yourself to Christ? It does not. How do we *know* that it does not? We may give the answer in the form of a question. When you give yourself entirely to Christ, which part of you is it which is expressing itself? It is the *deepest* in you. When you afterward fall into sin, even if at the moment you do it wilfully, which part of you is it *then* which is expressing itself? Is it the *deepest* in you? No;

it is the *weakest*. Does that which is weakest cancel out that which is *deepest* in you? Not at all. You need not keep having to re-enact the *transaction* of getting yourself to the point of uttermost yieldedness. Confess at once the sin you have committed, or the wrong attitude you have allowed, and humbly claim cleansing through the precious blood of Christ. Thus there is immediate restoration. The point is: there need not be a repeated re-enacting of the basic, decisive crisis of entire consecration to Christ, but there can be (and will be) a continual *renewing of the covenant* which you then made with Him. In other words, consecration is both a decisive crisis and a continuing day-by-day endorsement.

Inwrought sanctification will not bring *sinlessness*, but it assuredly brings true *holiness*. There are those who argue that unless there is absolute sinlessness there is not true holiness; but they are wrong. By way of parallel, in the physical human body there is nowhere an *absolute* non-existence of disease, for absolute health would be immortality. Yet there *can* be abounding good health. And what abounding good health is, in the *body*, inwrought holiness is to the *soul*. That wonderful chapter on love, 1 Corinthians 13, is not a description of sinlessness, but it *is* a photograph of true *holiness*; and that very love may be "shed abroad in our hearts by the Holy Spirit" (Rom. 5: 5). "Love is the fulfilling of the law" (Rom. 13: 10). Is not *that* holiness? "He that *dwelleth* in love dwelleth in God, and *God in Him*" (1 John 4: 16). Is not *that* holiness?

Let the mind be kept mainly on this highest and most *positive* aspect of holiness—the infilling love of God. To be continually raising questions on the *negative* aspects, i.e. as to what *degree* we may be freed from sin, tends to be aggravating rather than edifying. The New Testament nowhere pledges a present absolute sinlessness to us, but it *does* set before us this true *holiness*, of which the sublimest aspect is the heart flooded with the love of God Himself.

Fellow-believer, if you should enter into this "goodly land" of entire sanctification, and the Holy Spirit should make it all "come alive" to you by gracious visitations of the "joy unspeakable", beware of that *subtlest* peril which can beset the sanctified, the liability to spiritual *pride*. God never indulges favouritism; but He loves humility. Beware of impatience with those whose inward eyes do not see what *you* see, and whose hearts do not have the experience which is *yours*.

Another counsel: Beware of what is known as "pathetic fallacy", a dictionary definition of which is, "the reading of one's own emotions into external nature". Beware of assuming that because *you* are intensely concerned with holiness, all *other* people are—either inside or outside the Church. You will probably have to live and work with folk who are not concerned one bit, and you will need to learn adjustment to this. True sanctification often has to live with those who misunderstand it, and sometimes with those who resent it, hate it, oppose it. Do not quail. It is under such circumstances that real sanctification finds its sweetest fellowship with Christ, and eventually sheds its most telling influence. How *can* we expect this spiritually blind world to understand sanctification? Even when the earth's Maker Himself walked its streets it did not recognise Him! God's Enochs have always walked the more closely with Him because they were misunderstood by the men of this world's "Vanity Fair".

But we will add no more, though further thoughts come crowding in. The inviting doorway to this "fulness of the blessing" is wide open to those who will enter. As we have said, the entrance-point is a whole-hearted self-yielding to Christ, accompanied by a reckoning on the divine promise. Listen again to that inviting guarantee in 1 Thessalonians 5: 23, 24.

"THE GOD OF PEACE HIMSELF SANCTIFY YOU WHOLLY; AND MAY YOUR WHOLE SPIRIT AND SOUL AND BODY BE PRESERVED BLAMELESS, TO THE COMING OF OUR LORD JESUS CHRIST. FAITHFUL IS HE THAT CALLETH YOU [TO THIS] *WHO ALSO WILL DO IT.*"

If God has to do some wrestling with that Jacob-nature of yours, let Him. Do not wrestle back. Do as Jacob did at Peniel: cling, and say, "I will not let Thee go unless Thou bless me". Sometimes, rather drastically, God has to break the thigh of our selfism, but always it is so that a limping Jacob may become a leaping Israel—"a prince with God". Those who really come into the blessing soon begin to know in a new way the spiritual meaning of Isaiah 60: 19, 20,

"The sun shall be no more thy light by day, neither for brightness shall the moon give light unto thee; but the LORD shall be unto thee an everlasting light, and thy God thy glory. Thy sun shall no more go down, neither shall thy moon withdraw itself; for the LORD shall be thine everlasting light, and the days of thy mourning shall be ended."

It is an axiomatic law of the spiritual life that we possess by *being* possessed. When I am *altogether* Christ's, He is altogether mine. When once we are *fully* His there is little need for "claiming". The Lord never leaves a surrendered vessel empty. The fourfold formula is: (1) What I give to Him, He *takes*; (2) what He takes He *cleanses*; (3) what He cleanses He *fills*; (4) what He fills He *uses*. Therefore, again in the words of Isaiah 60,

"ARISE, SHINE; FOR THY LIGHT IS COME, AND THE GLORY OF THE LORD IS RISEN UPON THEE."

Addendum 1: *Excursus on the Etymology of Sanctification*

USING the King James (or Authorized) Version, we find that the word, "sanctification", occurs in our New Testament 5 times; "sanctified", 16 times; "sanctifieth" 4, and "sanctify" 6. In each of these 31 instances the Greek word is either a noun or verb form of the Greek adjective, *hagios* (which is true also in the English Revised Version and the American Standard Version).

On looking up that Greek word, *hagios*, we find that it occurs in the New Testament (including its noun and verb variants) 278 times, translated as follows:

"holy"	167	"sanctifieth"	4
"holiness"	9	"sanctify"	6
"holiest"	3	"saints"	62
"sanctification"	5	"sanctuary"	4
"sanctified"	16	"hallow"	2

So, if we would rightly apprehend what sanctification is, we must know two things about that Greek word, *hagios*: (a) its meaning etymologically, (b) its usage Scripturally.

As to its etymology, there is little doubt that its primary force is that of *separatedness*—as the separatedness of a victim for religious sacrifice, or of temple utensils, priests, devotees. But outgrowing from that is the further meaning of *sacredness*, for by reason of their separatedness sacrificial victims and temple utensils and consecrated devotees are different from all others. The final meaning, especially in Jewish and Christian orientation, is *purity in character*: the separated lamb must be "without blemish", the separated appurtenances of the temple must be specially "cleansed", the separated *person* must be purified by prescribed ablutions and must also exhibit outstanding godliness of life. In New Testament teaching concerning the sanctification of Christian believers, it is that third meaning which has main emphasis, i.e. *purity of character*.

There are those who more or less *limit* the word to that first idea of separatedness, but they err in so doing. The excellent Dr. Ironside, for instance, in his book already quoted, says, "Freed from all theological accretions; the naked verb, 'to sanctify', means *to set apart*, and the noun, 'sanctification', means, literally, *separation*" (p. 48).

For exegetical purposes it is always good to get back, through etymology to root meanings. Yet when we so rigidly adhere to this as to ignore the common usage of a word, we often blunder. As Dr. William Evans used to say, "Etymology apart from context slays us. Context along with etymology saves us." Etymology by itself can stultify rather than clarify.

Thus, a little later, Dr. Ironside, clinging to the "naked" etymology of *hagios*, seems quite decidedly to exclude any possibility of our being "wholly sanctified" in an *inwrought* sense by the Holy Spirit through the written Word, for he adds: "If sanctification in its practical sense be by the Word, I shall never be wholly sanctified in this aspect of it until I know that Word perfectly and am violating it in no particular. And that will never be on earth" (p. 68). Yet while Dr. Ironside says, "I shall never be *wholly sanctified*" (in a "practical" sense by the "Word") Paul prays, "The very God of peace *sanctify you wholly*" (1 Thess. 5: 23) plainly meaning experiential or "practical" sanctification of our "whole spirit and soul and body"!

Let it be at once agreed and underscored that *hagios* certainly does mean this set-apartness. Yet that must not be allowed to curtain off its further, richer meanings relating to experience and character. Some 94 times the New Testament names the third Member of the Godhead the "Holy Spirit", each time using the neuter of *hagios*. Does it mean no more than "the set-apart Spirit"? Over and over the word is used with an ethical and moral and spiritual content, e.g. 1 Peter 1: 15, "As He who called you is holy, be ye yourselves also holy in all manner of living". Are we to understand therefrom no more than, "As God is set apart, be ye also set apart"? When Romans 7: 12 says, "The Law is holy and righteous and good", does it mean no more than "The Law is set apart"? Does *hagios* mean no more than set apart in Ephesians 5: 27, "A glorious Church, not having spot or wrinkle or any such thing, but that it should be holy [or sanctified] and without blemish". All the many such verses indicate that sanctification or holiness in a Christian sense means an inward, moral, spiritual *purity*.

Some Classifications

If, now, we look through all those New Testament verses which refer to the sanctification of *Christian believers,* we soon find them grouping into significant classification. Apart from the 62 instances where *hagios* in the singular or plural is translated as "saint" or "saints" there are 52 occurrences in which its noun or verb or adjective forms refer to the sanctification of Christian believers. These group themselves into several classes representing different aspects of sanctification. There are those which emphasize that sanctification is a *divine* activity toward or within Christian believers (1 Cor. 1: 30, Heb. 2: 11). There are others which just as clearly indicate a *human* side to it (2 Cor. 7: 1, 2 Tim. 2: 21). There are passages which make it a once-for-all sanctification (2 Thess. 2: 13, Heb. 10: 10); whereas others seem to make it a progressive development in the believer (Rom. 12: 1, 2, Heb. 12: 14). There is the *corporate* sanctification of a whole church or body (Acts 20: 32; 26: 18, 1 Cor. 1: 2); and there is also the sanctification of believers *individually* (Col. 3: 12; Eph. 1: 4; 1 Pet. 1: 15).

A basically important feature to observe is that all these 52 references to the sanctification of believers break into two main categories: (1) *positional* sanctification, (2) *experiential* sanctification. The former is objective: something wrought *for* the believer by God through Christ. The latter is subjective: something wrought *in* the believer by God the Holy Spirit.

Addendum 2: *Excursus on "Positional" Sanctification*

Our omniscient God and Father, who knows from before the beginning of time all the saved in Christ, has in a once-for-all sense *set apart* or "sanctified" them in a *positional* sense.

In Acts 20: 32, we find, "And now I commend you to God, and to the word of His grace, which is able to build you up and to give you an inheritance among all those *having been* sanctified". We have the same in chapter 26: 18, "those *having been* sanctified". In both verses the verb is the perfect tense participle, indicating an already completed act pertaining to all Christian believers.

In 1 Corinthians 1: 2, we read, "Unto the church of God which is at Corinth, *having been* sanctified in Christ Jesus". It is that perfect tense again; an already completed divine act of sanctifying. Some of those Corinthian believers were far from exhibiting "entire sanctification" in their daily life and behaviour, as the epistle exposes; yet they were *positionally* sanctified (set apart) in Christ. In that sense, just as truly as they were *justified* in Him, despite their personal unrighteousness, so they were positionally *sanctified* in Him, despite their individual unholiness.

The same is reasserted, with fuller meaning, in verse 30: "But of Him [God] are ye in Christ Jesus, who *was made* [aorist] unto us wisdom from God, even righteousness and sanctification and redemption." Mark well our new standing before God, i.e. "in Christ Jesus", and that He "was made" (not *will* be, or is now *being* made) our sanctification. Our new *standing*, as Christian believers is that of sanctification in Christ. Of course, this particular verse has further outreaches, but its primary reference is to the *positional*.

So is it in chapter 6: 11, in which we find three past tenses going together: "But ye *were* washed, ye *were* sanctified, ye *were* justified." So sanctification was effected synchronically with justification. Exactly as justification was immediate and perfect through the vicarious righteousness of Christ, so was our positional sanctification through His imputed holiness.

Even more clearly this positional sanctification flashes out from Hebrews 10: 10, "By which will [of God] we *have been* sanctified through the offering of the body of Jesus Christ once for all." As the offering was "once for all", so is the sanctification which it effected for us—which clearly must mean sanctification *positionally* in Christ. So too is it in verse 29.

See also Colossians 3: 12, "Put on therefore, as God's elect, holy [or sanctified ones] and beloved, a heart of compassion, kindness, lowliness. . . ." In other words, our *position* as sanctified ones is to be reflected in all our behaviour.

Finally, let it be well observed that this positional sanctification was actualised by the Holy Spirit at our conversion. 1 Peter 1: 2 says, "Elect . . . according to the foreknowledge of God the Father, in [or by] sanctification *of the Spirit,* unto obedience and sprinkling of the blood of Jesus Christ". (See also 2 Thessalonians 2 : 13, 14.)

Such are the leading New Testament references to the *positional* sanctification of Christian believers. Perhaps the following simple abstract may usefully crystallise them :

1. It is by election of God the Father (1 Pet. 1 : 2, Heb. 10 : 10).
2. It is through union with God the Son (1 Cor. 1 : 2 and 1 : 30).
3. It is actualised by the Holy Spirit (2 Thess. 2 : 13, 1 Pet. 1 : 2).
4. It is coincident with justification (1 Cor. 6 : 11, Acts 26 : 18).
5. It covers all believers collectively (Acts 20 : 32, 26 : 18).
6. It is once-for-all, perfect for ever (Heb. 10 : 10, 14, 2 Thess. 2 : 13).

EXCURSUS ON THE WORD "PERFECT"

Of the seven different words translated as "perfect" in our New Testament, the standard is τέλειος (in English, teleios), which occurs forty times, though only sixteen of the forty occurrences refer to human condition. Its intrinsic meaning is that of being complete, fulfilled, or full-grown. For instance, Epictetus, in his *Encheiridion,* encouraging his disciples to live as true philosophers, says, "No longer art thou a stripling, but a man forthwith full-grown (*teleios*). Forthwith, therefore, have thyself live as full-grown (*teleios*), and as one who is pressing forward." It is interesting that one of the earliest Anglo-Saxon translations of "Be ye perfect" in Matthew 5 : 48 is *Beothfulfremede,* that is, "Be ye full-framed".

I do not deny that the Greek word *can* mean absolute perfection, for both it and our English word, "perfect", can be used in either a relative or absolute sense ; the immediate context must decide. In the New Testament, *teleios,* when used of present Christian possibility is used only in a relative sense. As Archbishop Trench says in his *Synonyms,* whenever Paul "employs the word in an ethical sense he does it continually with this image of full, *completed growth,* as contrasted with infancy and childhood". As plainly as can be, therefore, when Dr. Hodge equates the holiness now required of us with utter absence of "defect or omission", he is confusing holiness with sinlessness, and blamelessness with faultlessness. He is setting the requirement higher than the New Testament itself does!

Books by J. Sidlow Baxter

Does God Still Guide?
Baxter offers insights into questions such as: Which is the right way? Is there a sure guide? Does God still guide? How may I know? Dr. Baxter sets forth a clear-cut presentation of biblical truth.
ISBN 0-8254-2199-3   192 pp.   paperback   8.99

The God You Should Know
J. Sidlow Baxter shows how ordinary people can come to grips with the most extraordinary reality of the Christian life, the God who is here in power, love, and majesty. Destined to rank among the Christian classics!
ISBN 0-8254-2174-8   256 pp.   paperback   9.99

Mark These Men
A treasure house of Bible biographies including Elisha, Elijah, King Saul, Daniel, Gideon, Balaam, and Nehemiah. Also included are New Testament characters such as the Apostle Paul, Lazarus, the rich young ruler, Ananias, Simon of Cyrene, and many others.
ISBN 0-8254-2197-7   192 pp.   paperback   9.99

The Strategic Grasp of the Bible
An extensive look into the origin, structure, and message of the Word of God. A condensed version of the author's exemplary work, *Explore the Book*.
ISBN 0-8254-2198-5   406 pp.   paperback   12.99

The "Christian Sanctification" Series

A New Call to Holiness
This volume examines the right approach to Scripture while guarding against the errors which have beguiled others in discussing the plain question, "What is holiness?" *A New Call to Holiness* is Volume One of the "Christian Sanctification Series."
ISBN 0-8254-2170-5   256 pp.   paperback   9.99

His Deeper Work in Us
Baxter explores the topic of holiness, answering questions such as: Does the Bible teach a deeper, further work of the Holy Spirit in the believer? Is there complete freedom from sin? *His Deeper Work in Us* is Volume Two of the "Christian Sanctification Series."
ISBN 0-8254-2172-1   256 pp.   paperback   9.99

Our High Calling
These devotional and practical studies affirm the need for personal sanctification, pointing to the New Testament's emphasis on the individual and the call to sanctification as "one of the most ringing of its imperatives." *Our High Calling* is Volume Three of the "Christian Sanctification Series."
ISBN 0-8254-2171-3   208 pp.   paperback   9.99